SEEING SOLOMON'S KNOT LOIS ROSE ROSE

seeing
SOLOMON'S KNOT

To Joyce —
Follow the wisp'
Lois Rose Rose
12/2/08

LOIS ROSE ROSE

seeing
SOLOMON'S KNOT

LIBRARY OF CONGRESS CONTROL NUMBER:
AVAILABLE ON REQUEST

ISBN 097776700-0

SAN 850-1009

To my dear grandchildren,
Ian Lipton and Grace Lipton,
to my darling daughter Sharon,
and to all who read this...

I wish Solomon's Knot,
this Grandfather of All Knots,
like your own Grandparents,
would always and forever
protect you,
inform you,
and help you see the things
that make you wise.

SEEING SOLOMON'S KNOT LOIS ROSE ROSE

the all—faith symbol of faith

SEEING SOLOMON'S KNOT LOIS ROSE ROSE

THE ALL—FAITH SYMBOL OF FAITH?

WHY?

BECAUSE FORMING SOLOMON'S KNOT DEMANDS INTELLIGENCE.

IT WAS, IT IS, UNDERSTOOD AS THE MARK OF WISDOM.

IT IS JUST THAT SIMPLE.

SEEING SOLOMON'S KNOT LOIS ROSE ROSE

contents

IMAGE 1
Hand screen printed by the author, the Knot in gold.
United States of America. 1981 C.E.

photography: Joel Lipton

SEEING SOLOMON'S KNOT LOIS ROSE ROSE

Introducing the author

NO EXPEDITION WAS MOUNTED, NO TENURE TRACK FOLLOWED, BUT FOR TWENTY FIVE YEARS SOLOMON'S KNOT JUST KEPT TURNING UP, EACH SIGHTING GIVING NEW DIMENSION TO THE LAST. THE PROCESS OF DISCOVERY HAS BEEN LIFE ENHANCING AND FUN. THE BOOK IS OFFERED IN THAT SPIRIT.

YOU WILL FIND OVER EIGHTY IMAGES OF SOLOMON'S KNOT, EACH AN EXAMPLE OF A DIFFERENT MANIFESTATION OF THE DESIGN. THE IMAGES ARE INTENDED TO PLEASE YOUR EYE, AND TO HELP YOU TO RECOGNIZE THE KNOT WHEN YOU FIND IT, AND YOU WILL FIND IT.

THERE IS TEXT INTENDED TO FULFILL THE DESCRIPTION OF THIS WORK AS A "READ ALOUD ART BOOK."

YOU WILL FIND POEMS, POEMS TO ENTERTAIN YOU OR TO MOVE YOU. HERE IS A PROPHECY: YOU WILL REMEMBER THE POEMS, THEY WILL HELP YOU TO UNDERSTAND THE "GRANDFATHER OF ALL KNOTS."

THERE IS AN EXTENSIVE ANNOTATED BIBLIOGRAPHY. THE REFERENCES FEATURED IN THE BIBLIOGRAPHY WILL CONCLUSIVELY ANSWER THE QUESTION OF WHETHER THE KNOT HAS BEEN INTERNATIONALLY RECOGNIZED, RECOGNIZED BY NAME, RECOGNIZED AMONG MANY FAITHS AS SIGNIFICANT NOW AND IN THE PAST.

AND THERE ARE PERSONAL ACKNOWLEDGEMENTS TO OFFER THANKS TO CONTRIBUTORS AND TO PROVIDE A SENSE OF THE DYNAMICS OF SEEING SOLOMON'S KNOT.

Lois Rose Rose

SEEING SOLOMON'S KNOT LOIS ROSE ROSE

Introducing the Knot

SOLOMON'S KNOT IS IN THE SCRIPTURES.

BEFORE YOU VIEW THE IMAGES, AN EXPLANATION OF THE CHOICES...

The Seal of Solomon on his magic ring,
the Star of David
and the Shield of that King,
all seem to be known with parity.
But the symbol I study,
Solomon's Knot,
is recognized only with rarity.
Since this book is intended
for many to use it,
there is nothing included
that just might confuse it
with anything else;
thus, for clarity
only Knot images,
so titled are shown
from examples worldwide,
but mainly my own,
well researched
and vetted for verity.

In the course of researching Solomon's Knot I have become aware that a great deal of attention, study, and debate have been directed toward two other symbols that are also often related to Jewish/Christian/Moslem/Eastern/Western history; they are the five pointed star and the six pointed star. The terms used to describe the stars are sometimes applied to Solomon's Knot as a sort of generic way to note that a symbol has a religious or mystical connotation.

Since one of the goals of this book is to provide a resource for artisans and scholars of all nations, and since the titles of the star symbols are a source of contention, I have decided not to include any images of them in this study, because they might be misinterpreted by those who do not or cannot read the English text.

For the same reason, for clarity, only the pure, basic form of Solomon's Knot is shown, knowing you will now have the information to recognize the many designs created by extending or elaborating upon the original Knot.

HAPPILY, SOLOMON'S KNOT SOLO HAS APPEARED IN SO MANY FORMS THAT ON ITS OWN IT OFFERS A RICH DESIGN REPERTOIRE, AS YOU WILL DISCOVER IN THE GALLERY

Solomon's Knot

F O R M S
U S E S

a gallery of photographs by
Joel Lipton

SEEING SOLOMON'S KNOT LOIS ROSE ROSE

PLATE I
The Philosopher's Classic Form Solomon's Knot.
Found object sculpture. Sherman Tank components.
Jim Robbins. United States of America. Late twentieth century C.E.
photography: Joel Lipton

SEEING SOLOMON'S KNOT LOIS ROSE ROSE

PLATE II
The Philosopher's Free Form Solomon's Knot.
Found object metal sculpture. Train track components.
Jim Robbins. United States of America. Late twentieth century C.E.
photography: Joel Lipton

PLATE III
Variations of Solomon's Knot on Ethiopian pendants.
Early twentieth century C.E.
photography: Joel Lipton

XV

SEEING SOLOMON'S KNOT LOIS ROSE ROSE

PLATE IV
Solomon's Knot engraved on a silver protective amulet, a "hamsa",
sometimes called "The Hand of Fatima."
Morocco. Early twentieth century C.E.

photography: Joel Lipton

SEEING SOLOMON'S KNOT LOIS ROSE ROSE

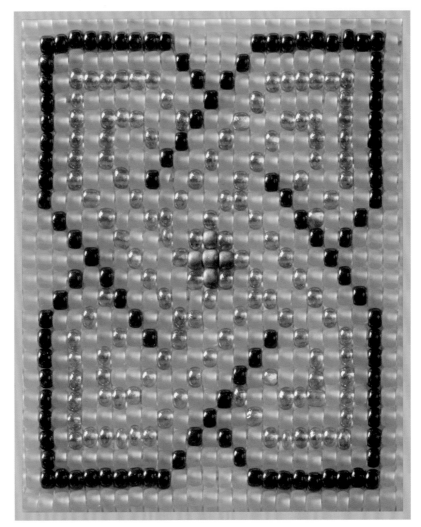

PLATE V
Solomon's Knot in glass beadwork.
Eva Walsh. United States of America. Late twentieth century C.E.
photography: Joel Lipton

SEEING SOLOMON'S KNOT LOIS ROSE ROSE

PLATE VI
Carved wood Divination Board with Solomon's Knots.
Ife People, Nigeria. Early twentieth century C.E.

photography: Joel Lipton

SEEING SOLOMON'S KNOT LOIS ROSE ROSE

PLATE VII
A glazed ceramic tile star radiates twelve Solomon's Knots.
Are they the incidental result of the
intricate interlacing that forms the star?
Is the star simply the result of the Knot interlaces?
Are the Knots stand-ins for the twelve astrological signs
that appear in some old synagogue art?
Spain. Late twentieth century C.E.

photography: Joel Lipton

PLATE VIII
Raku glazed clay vase with openwork Solomon's Knot.
Becca Licha. United States of America. Early twenty first century C.E.
photography: Joel Lipton

PLATE IX
Embroidered wool Moslem cap or Jewish kepah?
To see the Solomon's Knots, squint.
Uzbekistan, twentieth century C.E.

photography: Joel Lipton

PLATE X
Solomon's Knot tooled on leather.
Zaire. Twentieth century C.E.

photography: Joel Lipton

SEEING SOLOMON'S KNOT LOIS ROSE ROSE

PLATE XI

Solomon's Knot motif in woven raffia Kasai velvet.
Kuba people, Africa. Mid-twentieth century C.E.

photography: Joel Lipton

PLATE XII
Solomon's Knot stone mosaic.
Italy. Twentieth century C.E.
photography: Joel Lipton

SEEING SOLOMON'S KNOT LOIS ROSE ROSE

KINGS 5:9
"GIVE THY SERVANT AN UNDERSTANDING HEART..."

KINGS 5:12
"...I HAVE GIVEN THEE A WISE AND AN UNDERSTANDING HEART..."

SEEING SOLOMON'S KNOT LOIS ROSE ROSE

1—the proportion

One sign of all faiths,
revealed, made or found,
Solomon's Knot
is to all beliefs bound.

Worked, tied or told,
the Knot and its story
respected, revered
as a symbol of glory.

Each Knot alone
links all to its kind,
as intelligence forged
in the soul of Man's mind.

SEEING SOLOMON'S KNOT LOIS ROSE ROSE

AS THE OBJECTS IN THE GALLERY DEMONSTRATE

⊠ SOLOMON'S KNOTS APPEAR AS INTERLACED LINKS.

⊠ SOLOMON'S KNOTS MAY BE ONE, TWO, OR THREE DIMENSIONAL.

⊠ THE LINKS MAY BE OF MATCHING OR CONTRASTING COLORS.

THERE ARE MANY POSSIBLE STYLES.
HERE ARE THE BASIC VARIATIONS:

IMAGE 2
classic form
Detail from an
African crown.

IMAGE 3
graduated "Js"
Ancient mosaic.
Israel.

IMAGE 4
mitered tips
Antique tile.
Italy.

IMAGE 5
straight tips
Japanese
textile.

IMAGE 6
with box interlaced
Nigerian style
textile print.

IMAGE 7
closed curves
Silver amulet.
Morocco.

3

THE PHILOSOPHER'S
POTION, PORTION, AND PROPORTION

Dip and chips and geometry,
not a usual combination,
but exactly how it came to me
a philosophical revelation.

Jim Robbins was my husband's friend from childhood. Appetizers at home, then out to dinner with Jim and his wife, Elaine, had been our happy habit. The progress of Jim's work as a found metal artist and of my study of Solomon's Knot were often part of our conversation. So it was that one evening in the late 1990s the Robbins's hostess gift to me was a classic Solomon's Knot made by Jim from old tank parts. I was thrilled and pronounced it the signature image for my book-in-perpetual-progress.

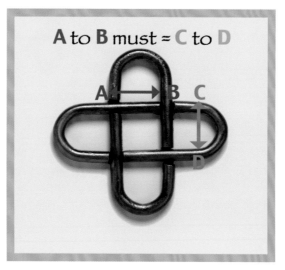

IMAGE 8
Philosopher's Classic Form Solomon's Knot.
photography: Joel Lipton

4

Four years later my dear husband had passed away, but dinner with Elaine and Jim continued as my custom. Jim was still fiddling around with the Knot, and one evening, with snacks at their house, he demonstrated to me that, in his words, "...any kid in a geometry class, given a pencil, a ruler, and a piece of string, would eventually discover this form." To create the Knot, rather than using two links interlaced, he analyzed the design as four identical J shaped units. He explained that the basic criterion for the J was the relationship of the span of the hook to the intersecting portion of the staff.

To demonstrate that the shape past the intersection was optional, he made another found metal sculpture. It had the classic Solomon's Knot proportion but had free form tops on the Js.

IMAGE 9
The Philosopher's Free Form Solomon's Knot.
photography: Joel Lipton

Later that night, home again following my instructive visit, I listened to a taped lecture on the history of philosophy. It was perfect timing. The focus of the lecture was the importance early civilizations placed on the ability to organize thought through mathematics. I realized that Jim's happy hour geometry lesson, the formation of a reliable, repeatable formula, had originally taken thousands of years to be envisioned, before there were pencils and rulers and string.

trim line

IMAGE 10

The following December, wanting personally to illustrate the Philosopher's Form theory, I decided to make the Js in my state-of-the-art graphics programs on my state-of-the-art computer. After spending hours each day for a week watching my Js do somersaults, bump one another around, or get permanently lost in some unreachable layer of *Photoshop* or *Illustrator* or *Quark*, I found just the Js that I needed among the holiday goodies at my local supermarket.

Mystics might call them *God's Rods*; I knew only that these candy canes, peppermint hooks on staffs, were about to become Solomon's Knots.

Scanned into my computer in the original proportion, the candy canes didn't quite fit to form a Knot, but with the staff of the canes trimmed to Jim's exact ratio, they gave sweet proof of the ancient formula.

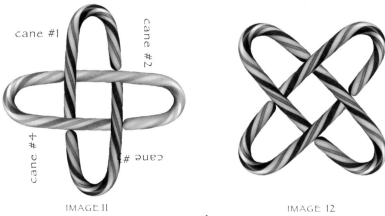

cane #1   cane #2

cane #4   cane #3

IMAGE 11   IMAGE 12

But, the original inspiration for the formula was not a confection, it was primal. In a study of a Central Asian Bronze Age site (circa the third millennium B.C.E.), **American** authors describe a Knot carved on a stone seal they found as an animal motif. **Russians** analyzing this same type of object describe two headed dragons. Illustrations from a **German** publication about archaeological finds in **Iran** and **Turkey** depict the interlace with snakes above two standing male figures, and adjacent to that picture is a drawing of a classic layered Knot. In **French** archives from ancient **Elam** (now **Iran**), there is a print of a stone carving showing two facing male figures turned toward the divinité snake interlace.

❀ WERE ENTWINED SNAKES THE EARLY INSPIRATION FOR THE KNOT? OR DRAGONS? OR THE MALE ORGAN?

❀ WHAT CULTURES SAW THIS SYMBOL AS DIVINE?

❀ WHAT CULTURES HAVE FORGOTTEN THIS SYMBOL?

❀ WHERE IS IT STILL NOTICED?

❀ WHO CALLS IT WHAT?

❀ WHY HAVE SOME NAMED IT AFTER SOLOMON?

❀ WHY IS SOLOMON TIED TO SOLOMON'S KNOT?

THE MOST COMPELLING REASON IS THAT THERE ARE ACTUALLY REFERENCES IN THE HEBREW SCRIPTURES TO THE KNOT IN THE FIRST TEMPLE, SOLOMON'S TEMPLE.

DESCRIBING THE DOORS TO THE NICHE THAT HOUSED THE ARK:

I Kings 6:18 "...the cedar upon the Temple on the inside was decorated with a network of designs of knots and open flowers..."

DESCRIBING THE BASIN, THE "SEA" THAT HELD WATER FOR RITUAL WASHING BY THE JEWISH PRIESTS:

I Kings 7:24 "Knots under its lip surrounded it..."
II Chronicles 4:2 "...bulls etched on knots..."

It should also be noted that translations in English may employ modern usage, or they may use Old English variants. One can find the consistent Hebrew word **PEKAIM** translated as "knot," "knob," or occasionally "knop," all of which are closely related to one another in English. But, in each case, whichever English word the old Rabbis and modern scholars chose to use for translation, the Hebrew word is **PEKAIM.**

"Open flowers" is the translation most often used for **I Kings 6:18** description of the design that, with Solomon's Knot, decorated the Ark. That design, like the Knot, symbolizes intellect and intent. The "open flowers" were likely rosettes composed of intersecting circles, the same combination of shapes that requires "...a pencil and a piece of string" to draw in a geometry class. A circle is by definition "perfect," it cannot be made unintentionally. Solomon's Knot and the circles of the "open flowers" are essentials of form. The circle that flowers with wisdom is a perfect companion for the Knot.

8

IMAGE 13
From a mosaic stone floor depicting the Ark with Solomon's Knots.
Bet Alpha Synagogue. Eretz Israel, sixth century C.E.

9

II—the concept

The Philosopher's Form demonstrates that Solomon's Knot can be constructed of four intersecting parts, but the Knot appears to be two interlacing links.

This section is devoted to looking beyond the structure of the symbol to find various influences that have shaped its powerful proportion.

The legends of the Knot are rich with layer upon layer of history recounted by generation after generation of storytellers. Solomon's Knot is simple in appearance, but complex with its many meanings. There is no need to understand it all at once. It is best to just read and look and enjoy. Comprehension will come.

TO LOOK AT SOLOMON'S KNOT LAYER BY LAYER

⊗ THINK KNOT, LOOP, LINK, CHAIN, CONTACT.

⊗ ADD ANOTHER DIMENSION, TIME.

⊗ INCLUDE ALL THE JEWISH READINGS OF THE BIBLE.

⊗ MIX IN ALL THE LEGENDS OF THE PEOPLE WHO KNOW THE HEBREW BIBLE STORIES IN ADDITION TO THEIR OWN.

⊗ CONSIDER THAT NO IRON WAS PERMITTED IN THE BUILDING OF THE TEMPLE, BUT SOLOMON WAS THE IRON AGE KING.

⊗ TAKE FROM THE TORAH THESE REFERENCES TO CHAINS, WHICH ARE INCLUDED, WITH THE KNOT, IN THE DESCRIPTIONS OF THE SACRED AREA OF THE ARK:

I Kings 6:21 "...he drew golden chains in front of the partition."

I Kings 7:17 "...ropes of chainwork..."

AND FURTHER IN THE HEBREW SCRIPTURES:

Chronicles 3:16 "...he made chains for the partition; he also put them on the tops of the pillars, and he made one hundred pomegranates, which he placed on the chains."

NOW ADD
THE FOLLOWING AFRICAN CREATION STORY,
TOLD TO ME BY A NIGERIAN IFE PRIEST...

African legend tells
of the God of Creation
sending First Man down to the World.
At that time before time,
the World was covered with water,
and First Man floundered and almost drowned,
but the God of Creation rescued him.
When First Man was given a second chance
to live in the World,
the God of Creation
lowered him from the Heavens
on an Iron chain.
The strength of the metal was Divine
and so the Iron links of the chain
provided First Man
with a direct connection
to the protection of his God.

- SEE THE ELEMENTS OF SOLOMON'S KNOT AS LINKS OF CHAIN, AS AN AFRICAN SYMBOL FOR THE BEGINNING OF LIFE ON EARTH.
- HONOR LINKS OF CHAIN AS AN AFRICAN SYMBOL FOR A CONNECTION TO A DIVINE FORCE.
- UNDERSTAND THE LINKS AS A SYMBOL FOR THE STRENGTH OF IRON, THE NATURAL SYMBOL FOR ALL METAL WORKERS AND MINERS, FROM THE SMITHS OF KING SOLOMON'S TIME TO THE CELTS WHO WORKED THE MINES OF EUROPE, TO THE ARTISANS OF THE NEW WORLD.
- CAST THE LINKS TO REPRESENT THE METAL OF COINS AND THE INTERPLAY OF COMMERCE AND THE SYMBOL TELLS OF BANKERS AND FINANCE.
- SENSE LINKS AS COUPLED, AND THEY REPRESENT DEVOTION AND PERPETUAL RENEWAL.
- BELIEVE THE LINKS OF A CHAIN TO BE WITHOUT BEGINNING AND WITHOUT END AND THEY ARE ETERNAL.

AFRICAN ROYALS RECOGNIZE THE ANCIENT POWER OF THE KNOT
AND USE A PERSONAL VARIATION FOR THEIR MAGICAL CROWNS.

IMAGES 14, 15, & 16
Glass beadwork Solomon's Knots on Yoruba crowns.
Africa, early to mid-twentieth century C.E.

photography: Lois Rose Rose

15

IMAGE 17
Solomon's Knot detail from the front panel of a Yoruba royal tunic.
Glass beads sewn individually onto woven cotton fabric.
Africa, early twentieth century C.E.

photography: Lois Rose Rose

The tunic that bears this Knot was originally part of a Yoruba chief's ceremonial dress. The original owner may also have had his variation of the Knot beaded onto his crown, his throne, and his royal footstool.

16

IMAGE 18
From Africa, old yellow powder glass Akoso beads
and newly made interpretations.

photography: Joel Lipton

The pairing of Solomon's Knot and beads
extends beyond beadwork done with glass
seedbeads, as shown on African royal crowns and
garments. Above, the Knot appears on larger glass
beads that are used for necklaces.

The older style yellow Akoso beads were made
from European glass shards ground up, heated to the
melting point and reformed. The decorative Knot
components were molded, then impressed in the
heated glass.

The newly made blue beads have the
decoration drizzled on and glazed. The craft
technique has changed but the sacred design
remains.

THIS CONNECTION BETWEEN AFRICA, THE KNOT AND THE HEBREW SCRIPTURES IS FOUND IN I Kings 10:1 AND II Chronicles 9:1 "The Queen of Sheba heard of Solomon's fame...."

As the Bible tells it, Makeda, the Queen of Sheba, found Solomon twice again as marvelous as she had been led to expect. He answered all her questions, she gave him gifts of rare spices and fabulous gems, she admired his palace and his court, and she went home.

As the Ethiopians tell it, after her visit to King Solomon, Makeda, the Queen of Sheba, returned to her realm and bore Solomon's son, Menelik. When Menelik reached manhood he traveled to Jerusalem to meet his father. For Menelik's journey home, Solomon provided as his guards the first born sons of his noblemen, and, the Ark of the Covenant. There is a claim that the Ark of the Covenant still resides in a small chapel in Aksum, Ethiopia; and Menelik, the Queen of Sheba's son by Solomon, is known as the first ruler of the Solomonic Dynasty in Ethiopia, a Dynasty that continued until 1974 C.E. when Hailie Selassie's reign was ended.

Unique to Ethiopia is the interpretation that the intertwined forms in the Knot represent Solomon and Makeda conceiving Menelik.

IMAGE 19
Detail from an Ethiopian pendant.

18

TO GIVE MORE MEANING TO THE EXAMPLES OF THE KNOT

THAT HAVE BEEN OFFERED IN THE PREVIOUS PAGES,

AND TO ENRICH THE EXPERIENCE OF DISCOVERING

THE IMAGES TO FOLLOW, HERE ARE THOUGHTS ON

SEEING SOLOMON'S KNOT

AS A PROGRESSION:

NOTICE

OBSERVE

UNDERSTAND

FEEL

To begin this progression, I reference the work of archaeologist Jonathan Mark Kenoyer from his study, *The Ancient Cities of the Indus Valley Civilization.* Kenoyer has a chapter about religious art and symbols that is thoughtful and richly documented. He declares that one way people seek to find order in their world is through religion. He then states that in the ancient Indus Valley Civilization religious ideas were expressed by symbols. He goes on to describe various types of symbols, public and personal, abstract and figural, including many references to knot motifs. It is an important addition to the literature of symbolism. But, it expresses the view of an expert observer in the COMMON ERA (C.E.)

The **C.E.** world is crowded with signs and signals and words, written, printed, recorded, transmitted across the surface of the earth, beneath the seas, and into the skies. Even during the time of the Indus Valley Civilization, to merit being called a Civilization there had to be man made objects and language and many, many symbols. The import of a single symbol in the ancient Indus Valley culture or the modern San Fernando Valley culture, or any other developed society, might be intuited, but hard to separate from the other visual clutter.

TO **SEE** THE ORIGINAL SYMBOLS,

GET BEYOND

NOTICE

BEYOND

OBSERVE

BEYOND

UNDERSTAND

TO

FEEL

TO FEEL A SYMBOL BEFORE THE COMMON ERA (B.C.E.)
A SYMBOL IN A WORLD FILLED ONLY WITH NATURE'S EXPRESSIONS,
THOUSANDS OF GENERATIONS BEFORE YOU AND ME AND THE INDUS
VALLEY CIVILIZATION, THE WORLD LONG, LONG BEFORE SOLOMON...

For eons no ion was known,
science not even imagined.
Darkness, light, warmth, and cold came and went,
and we shivered or sweated or saw or not
and didn't even wonder.
We fell or we drowned
with no memory, no warning.
We had yet to learn what we could eat
or what would eat us.
Birth was a mystery, death a puzzlement.
Then time revealed shape.
Patterns were discerned. Being recognized.
The perpetual quake of confusion
began to subside.
Came the need to define,
to record, to communicate.
Meaning, now there was meaning.
No longer confusion.
With meaning, understanding, then control.
Reliable, repeatable control.
Safety. Grab it. Don't lose it. Remember it.
Speak a word. Make a sign. Create a symbol.
Amid the yet unmarked rocks and sands
and forests of the planet and the mind,
symbols stood for all,
signaling intelligence, anticipating wisdom.

III—the story

IT IS AN AMAZING EXPERIENCE, COMPLETELY UNEXPECTED, IN THIS TIME OF OTHER PEOPLE'S EXPONENTIALLY EXPANDING VOLUMES OF INFORMATION, TO FIND MYSELF WITH SOMETHING TO SHARE THAT HAS NOT ALREADY BEEN EXTENSIVELY EXAMINED AND PUBLISHED.

IT *SEEMED* TO BEGIN LIKE THIS...

It walked into my studio.
It met me in New York.
It showed itself in Israel
and Spain
and County Cork.
It turned up in my home
via the Internet
and mail.
It came right in with friends
as a very small detail.
And so I'm in possession
of a scholarly obsession
with a Knot whose name is
Solomon, Celtic, or Nigerian,
an interlace with history
Hebraic and Iberian.
Its story has been elusive,
but my research is conclusive,
at least until new sightings sought
are found
and each demands new thought.

23

"it walked into my studio"

...in 1981, carried by a member of Los Angeles Mayor Tom Bradley's task force for the *Treasures of Ancient Nigeria* exhibition about to open at a local museum. She had heard that my mother, Bea Cole, and I had a small silk screen studio where we designed and printed custom items on textiles for museum stores.

Our visitor brought with her artifacts that had been collected while the task force was in Africa making arrangements for the exhibition. They wanted to have them adapted for sale at the host museum's shop. Among the items was a sample of a design that was referred to as the "Nigerian" Knot. The needlepoint kits that we printed from that prototype included that title.

IMAGE 20

The Knot, hand screen printed on cotton canvas by the author.
Adapted and needlepointed with tapestry wool by Bea Cole.
Los Angeles, California. 1981 C.E.

photography: Joel Lipton

24

"it met me in New York"

...introduced to me as Solomon's Knot by Samuel Kurinsky. Since 1984, at the suggestion of a store manager of a Jewish museum, I had been researching the Jewish connection to bead history. When I learned of Sam's book, *The Glassmakers, an Odyssey of the Jews*, I contacted him at his home in Brooklyn. He was glad to be found by someone doing simpatico research, and, taking his welcome seriously, my husband and I traveled to New York and spent a week studying with him. We turned our hotel suite into a projection room, and we were treated to a slide show that illustrated how Sam had become aware of the hidden Jewish experience in Italy.

While conducting his glass research in Altare, at the request of a local Catholic priest, Sam examined a nearby landmark Cathedral. Using the motifs found in the structure's original mosaic floors, which the priest called Solomon's Knots, plus his knowledge of Jewish history and classic synagogue design, Sam deduced that the Cathedral had been built on the foundation and mosaic floors of an early synagogue.

I recognized the Solomon's Knot in Italy as the same design that I originally screen printed as an African motif. I wondered if it might tell something about connections between Semitic and African creativity.

"it showed itself in Israel"

I began my first day in Israel with a visit to the Eretz Israel Museum in Tel Aviv. The museum is located on the site of an excavated settlement mound, with twelve separate pavilions, each featuring a different aspect of three thousand years of material culture in the area.

On my way into the museum I stopped at the museum store because a friend told me that they sold a craft kit to make a small mosaic Solomon's Knot. Indeed they did, but when I asked the store manager for information about the design and what it would be properly called in Hebrew, she knew only that it was a popular item and sold well.

Onward to the Pavilion of Glass. It was just receiving the finishing touches of a remodel, and though the exhibits were installed, it was still closed to the public. However, the supervising architect very kindly permitted me a quick walk around the displays, which were filled with ancient glass vessels and glorious beads. Before I was halfway around the exhibit I had acquired an entourage of curious curators. Noting how thrilled I was to see their wonderful material and interested in developing their own awareness of the significance of beads, they invited me into their shared office for a visit. That visit was the perfect beginning for my trip, with only one small disappointment.

As I was leaving them, I asked whether they were familiar with Solomon's Knot. They didn't recognize the term, so I drew a quick sketch, not a great sketch, but clear enough, and they didn't recognize that either.

My disappointment became bemusement when, a short distance from the Pavilion of Glass, not far from the museum store, I came upon an open air Mosaic Floor Exhibit. Variations of Solomon's Knot were the main design element in most of the segments of ancient mosaic stone floors on display. Brass plaques proposed them to be from a sixth century C.E. Samaritan house of worship and a sixth century C.E. site at Bet Guvrin, probably a monastery. Would attention to the complex history of the Knot motif have given a more complete understanding of the original purpose of the structures that housed these floors?

IMAGES 21 & 22
Solomon's Knots in mosaic floors.
Eretz Israel Museum, Tel Aviv. Israel
photography: Lois Rose Rose

"and Spain"

...in an antiques shop in Seville I purchased a tile simply because I found it attractive. Let me amend that...I **thought** I purchased a tile because I found it attractive, but now it seems possible that I purchased that tile because I had already started the hunt for Solomon's Knot, I just didn't know it yet. When I returned to my home in Los Angeles I packed all my travel trophies away and didn't look at them again for several years. By then I was very involved with researching the Knot and was a bit mystified to come upon a treasure that, earlier, I had felt so drawn to and unaccountably compelled to collect.

IMAGE 23
Ceramic tile with Solomon's Knot motif. Spain, fourteenth century C.E.
photography: Joel Lipton

"and County Cork"

IMAGE 24
Metal earrings with *Solomon's Knots*.
Late twentieth century C.E. Ireland.
photography: Joel Lipton

...in Ireland, land of the Celtic knot. On my first visit there I tried to find a pure Solomon's Knot among the myriad elaborate interlaces that typify the famous Celtic knots, but I had little success. The only example I found was the souvenir pair of earrings pictured here. Since great quantities of complex knot images were for sale everywhere, I quite wrongly deduced that the pure sample I had purchased was a fluke and had no real place in Irish history.

I held that belief until I saw a video of *Lord of the Dance*, a celebration of Irish custom and dance. About half way through the video I thought I was hallucinating because the entire male chorus of dancers appeared, each man wearing a black T-shirt with a single large gold Knot printed across the chest. Assured by my companions that they saw it, too, I tried to understand what the Knot represented in this context. Had the single essential Knot been used because it could be seen more clearly by the audience, or, since the dancers in this sequence seemed to be aggressors, did it represent an ancient feud or invasion? Was I seeing history, legend, or simply savvy costuming?

On my next trip to Ireland I looked in libraries instead of tourist shops (and pubs) and found that Irish art experts know the ancient Knot originated in the East, then traveled intact with the Celts across Europe, planting and gathering elaborate variations as it moved from artist to artist, until it found its ultimate home in Ireland.

AT THIS POINT I BEGAN TO

THINK OF SOLOMON'S KNOT AS

"The Grandfather of All Knots"

"it turned up in my home via the internet"

Searching for Solomon on the Internet yields a weird mixture of biblical quotations, mythical magical potions, botanical offerings, and occasionally an informed reference such as one posted by a group of Italian architects and mathematicians. Their posting honors Cosimo de' Medici's tombslab. The tombslab is inlaid with a Solomon's Knot of precious stones. Knowing the significance of Solomon's Knot through the Philosopher's Form makes it possible to understand at least one reason for the Knot marking the memorial of the great Florentine patron of Art and Science, and why it still attracts artists and scientists.

IMAGE 25
Solomon's Knot in the tombslab of
Cosimo de' Medici (1389-1464), Florence Italy.

IMAGE 26

Solomon's Knot on a souvenir replica of the city flag of Venice, Italy.

photography: Joel Lipton

In 1990 I purchased a replica of the old city flag of Venice from a street (canal) vendor. It is decorated with a Solomon's Knot.

- IS SOLOMON'S KNOT ON A VENETIAN BANNER AN EXTENSION OF FLORENTINE MEDICI HERALDRY?

- IS IT A CHURCH REFERENCE TO THE HEBREW SCRIPTURES?

- DOES IT SIGNIFY BANKING? ETERNITY? POWER?

- WAS I SIMPLY MISINFORMED BY THE CANAL VENDOR?

Italy's history raises questions that go back to the times of the Roman Empire's conquest and assimilation of various Barbarians, the era of the Crusades, the conflicts of the City States, the rising power of the Catholic Church and the ever present Jewish population.

I wonder about the presence of Solomon's Knot on the flag of Venice because the website of The National Gallery, London, England has an image of a fifteenth century C.E. painting titled *The Battle of San Romano*. The battle between San Romano and Florence took place in 1432. The text that accompanies the Internet display includes the statement that the victorious leader of the Florentine forces, Niccolo da Tolentino, is identifiable by Solomon's Knot on his banner.

Does *da Tolentino* in Italian speak of *de Toledo* in Spanish? Is a Spanish heritage the reason the Knot identifies the soldier, Niccolo? Or was it his allegiance to the Florentine Medici family? Or, it must be asked again, does the Knot have a more general meaning?

Renaissance Venice was a hub for banking, trade, and trade goods manufacture. When politics permitted, Jews were involved in all those endeavors. Today the Women's Gallery of the Sephardic Synagogue in Venice, the Scoula la Leventina, built about 1700 C.E., has a stained glass window featuring Solomon's Knot. Solomon's Knot is also found on plaques in the old Jewish cemetery near the Leventina Synagogue.

Since the Knot was used in Spain centuries before the Inquisition and the subsequent Expulsion of the Sephardim, perhaps it reflects the Spanish Exile history of the Leventina congregation, and the personal history of Niccolo da Tolentino.

33

"and mail"

Karlis Karklins and Robert Liu
BEADS and ORNAMENT, "Thank you!"
for making Solomon's Knot hot,
because before now it was not.

This **"Thank you!"** began my presentation about Solomon's Knot to the Society of Bead Researchers at International Bead Expo in Santa Fe, New Mexico in 2002. I had special thanks to offer, (besides my daily blessing upon both these great researcher/writers,) because days before I had received the current editions of *Ornament Magazine* and *Beads, the Journal of the Society of Bead Researchers*. Each magazine had a cover story featuring African powder glass Akoso beads, the beads that are traditionally decorated with Solomon's Knots. The photos showed demonstrations of the beads being made.

The articles also demonstrated the uncanny good fortune that has smiled upon this study, and they added a bonus that I had never considered: they made the Solomon's Knot study timely to the point of being almost trendy!

"it came right in with friends, as a very small detail"

Friends Stella and Fred Krieger came to my home with the gift of a book, *Mexican Silver*, in which jewelry from their collection was featured. While fabulous jewelry was the story, for me the stand-out was the frontispiece which featured an illustration from the fifteenth century C.E. *Codex Mendoza*. It included a silversmith's brazier with Solomon's Knot issuing from the flames. Upon inquiry, I learned that Solomon's Knot has long been the traditional symbol for metalsmiths in Mexico.

Years later I had the pleasure of entertaining a scion of the Taxco silversmithing family, Los Castillo. I showed him the notes for this book. He commented that his father had made earrings using the Knot motif. He was also familiar with the Knot as a symbol for metal workers in Mexico.

Then he asked me, *"Why do you follow Solomon's Knot?"*

I replied, *"I don't follow Solomon's Knot; Solomon's Knot comes to me, just as you have come right into my home bringing still more of the Knot's tradition with you."*

IMAGES 27 A & 27 B
Single glazed ceramic tiles. Italy. Eighteenth century C.E.

At twilight, during an annual Antiques Fair in Rome, when the elegant shop lined Via del Coronari glows with torch lights, I came upon the tile showroom of Signor Muffatone. There I saw these individual hand painted tiles. The charismatic owner said they were taken from the ruins of an old villa in Tivoli and that he had only a few more of each design. The single tiles were Interesting, but I had no need for them. I browsed a bit more, listening to the romantic *fado* music playing in the background; then I left.

"and each demands new thought"

The next day, even after admitting to myself that it was probably the charm of the owner and/or the enchanting tapes he played, I went back to the shop to "see the rest of the tiles." Muffatone was still charming, the music was still romantic, but when I saw the full sets of these tiles, I knew the real reason that I returned. The process remains a mystery to me.

COMPLETED, EACH SET OF FOUR TILES
BECAME A SOLOMON'S KNOT!
HOW COULD I POSSIBLY HAVE ANTICIPATED THAT SIGHTING?

IMAGES 28 A & 28 B
Solomon's Knot in four parts. Glazed ceramic tiles.
Italy. Eighteenth century C.E.
photography: Joel Lipton

IV—confirmation

Before I could say
I had to see
the pattern of this mystery.
Before I could write
I had to know
the truth of what I had to show.
I believed that I could find the clues
in my beads, my books, the news.
With each find, the picture developed
of ancient movements
and cultures enveloped.
But what does it mean?
Is a story told here?
I think so,
reflections on tales held dear.

"in my beads"

IMAGE 29
Solomon's Knot as a gilded glass bead. Circa 1939 C.E.
photography: Joel Lipton

This gilded black glass bead, molded in the shape of Solomon's Knot, was made by a Czech beadmaker before World War II. I purchased it from a bead dealer who specializes in vintage glass beads. She has made many trips to Europe, buying beads that were found in warehouses closed during the Holocaust. She told me that most of the people she originally dealt with in Czechoslovakia and Germany were Jews whose families had been in the bead business for generations.

Presumably those families dealt with people of many beliefs, and the beads they made sometimes represented various religious symbols, such as stars or stars and crescents, to satisfy their diverse market.

Was this bead intended for the African market? The Moslem market? The Jewish market? Or does it symbolize the Jewish glassmaking, beadmaking, heritage of the beadmaker?

"my books"

IMAGE 30
From a manuscript. Italy. Fourteenth century C.E.
graphic adaptation: Lois Rose Rose

Among my books, medieval manuscripts, rich with images. Pictured here, a detail from the Vatican commissioned *Treatise on the Vices*. It depicts financial lenders conducting business. Their religious identity is suggested by their laripippes, a typical Jewish hat of the period, and by the Hebrew writing in the account books.

※ IS THEIR BANKING TRADE PROCLAIMED BY THE SERIES OF SOLOMON'S KNOTS ON THE WALL BEHIND THEM?

※ OR ARE THE KNOTS INTENDED AS FURTHER RELIGIOUS IDENTIFICATION?

"the news"

Solomon's Knot in the news arrived on my doorstep in June, 2001, pictured in the Los Angeles Times. A report of a funeral in Jerusalem included a picture of a young man wearing a kepah banded by a series of Solomon's Knots. A kepah is a cap traditionally worn by Jewish men and boys. This cap may have been made for the young man by a needleworking friend or relative, or, since many of the great needleworkers are men, the young man in the photo may have sewn it himself. The pattern for the cap was probably found in a pattern book for embroidery and needlepoint featuring Judaic motifs. For example a book published in New York in 1979 shows the stitchery pattern for the knot and refers to it as *KIng Solomon's Knot*.

IMAGE 31

Solomon's Knot motif on ring purchased by the author
at the museum store of the Musee du Louvre, Paris, France.

photography: Joel Lipton

Solomon's Knots are found on ornament and in mosaic floors at sites in what are now France and Germany.

The information that came with this ring, featuring a Solomon's Knot motif, which I purchased at the Louvre, states that the design was taken from a Merovingian period medallion found in Charney, France at the site of an old Roman road. The ring was shown on the cover of the Louvre's museum store catalog. The catalog's citation mentioned that the ring's motif was adapted from circular gold-leaf pendants that were in fashion in the second half of the 6th century C.E. The citation went on to state that the pendants were often associated with glass beads, beads that often had millefiori designs.

WHO WORE SUCH FINERY, WHO MADE SUCH DECORATIONS?

⚛ THE CELTS, WITH THEIR INTERLACES, WERE IN THE AREA.

⚛ THE REFERENCE TO GLASS AND BEAD MAKING SUGGESTS A JEWISH PRESENCE, OR JEWISH MADE OR TRADED GOODS, SINCE JEWISH GLASSMAKERS TOOK THE MILLEFIORI TECHNIQUE TO EUROPE FROM THE MIDDLE EAST.

⚛ PLINY, THE ELDER, CENTURIES EARLIER, NOTED THE FONDNESS OF JEWISH WOMEN FOR BEADS.

⚛ SOLOMON'S KNOT IS FOUND AT SYNAGOGUE SITES OF THE ROMAN PERIOD.

These seemingly random facts may come together to contribute to understanding the meaning of the Knot in a Merovingian setting. The Jewish experience during that period is the one that has been least considered, so perhaps it still holds undiscovered information, information to explain who fashioned the original objects that inspired the ring I purchased at the Louvre, or who made a metal pendant disc found at a Merovingian site in Deutsche-Krottingen, a disc that has a Solomon's Knot at its center. And, the long over due "new" history, the academically credited scholarly exploration of the day to day life of commoners rather than courtiers or conquerors, may be what reveals the identity of the artisans who mined the stone, cut the tessera and laid the Solomon's Knot covered mosaic floor at Seviac, a first millennium C.E. excavated villa in Southwestern France.

"and tales held dear"

The domain of the Queen of Sheba was influenced by Africa, South and North of the Sahara. Her fabled trip to Jerusalem to meet King Solomon is the perfect metaphor for the cultural exchange that occurred in that region through trade, conquest, political interaction, and the basic tendency of people to imitate or acquire that which they admire.

Perhaps Solomon's Knot first traveled between Jewish and African cultures at the point in history that we have noted, when these two monarchs met.

Are Sheba and King Solomon the nexus of this puzzle that continues to perplex us?

IMAGE 32
Table covering with embroidered Solomon's Knot.
Ethiopia. Late twentieth century C.E.

photography: Joel Lipton

45

V—in all its fashions

What exists but seems not seen
on tombstones and Torahs
and a Lady, but briefly, an English Queen?
It's a riddle telling of varied passions,
the essential Knot in all its fashions.

"on tombstones"

IMAGES 33
Solomon's Knot in the mausoleum of the
Home of Peace Cemetery, Los Angeles, California.
Established at the beginning of the twentieth century,
it is one of the oldest Jewish cemeteries in the area.
The mausoleum was built in 1934.
photography: Lois Rose Rose

Solomon's Knot is the primary design motif in the mausoleum of the *Home of Peace Cemetery* in East Los Angeles. It appears molded in cement and carved in stone on arches and entryways throughout the tomb's structure.

The Wilshire Boulevard Temple is the synagogue that administers the cemetery. Its records indicate that, when the mausoleum was built, Solomon's Knot was understood to signify Eternity.

"and Torahs"

Dramatic evidence of the historical identification of Solomon's Knot with Judaism is found in the Knot's appearance on the Torah of one of Judaism's most revered scholars, Maimonides; and on the first bible printed for the Sephardic Jewish community.

IMAGE 34

Solomon's Knot on the Jerusalem Mishnah Torah.
The original of this Torah belonged to the revered scholar, Maimonides.
This Torah was copied in Spain and
illuminated in Perugia, Italy, circa 1400.C.E.

IMAGE 35

Solomon's Knots on the cover of the
first Hispano/Portuguese bible.
Late fifteenth century C.E.

49

"and a Lady, but briefly, an English Queen"

A full length portrait of Lady Jane Grey, the hapless adolescent who was nominally Queen of England for just nine days, shows her magnificently dressed in a gown with Solomon's Knots embroidered in pearls on the sleeves and skirt. The painting is dated circa 1545 C.E. Given the painting's context, the Solomon's Knots raise these questions...

- **WERE THE KNOTS PURELY DECORATIVE?**
- **WERE THEY SYMBOLS OF PRESTIGE OR WEALTH?**
- **WERE THEY INTENDED TO BE PROTECTIVE AMULETS?**
- **OR, SINCE BOTH THE PEARL INDUSTRY AND THE NEEDLE ARTS WERE AREAS OF ACTIVE JEWISH PARTICIPATION DURING THIS PERIOD, DID THESE SOLOMON'S KNOTS HAVE SPECIAL MEANING TO THE ARTISAN WHO DID THE STITCHERY?**

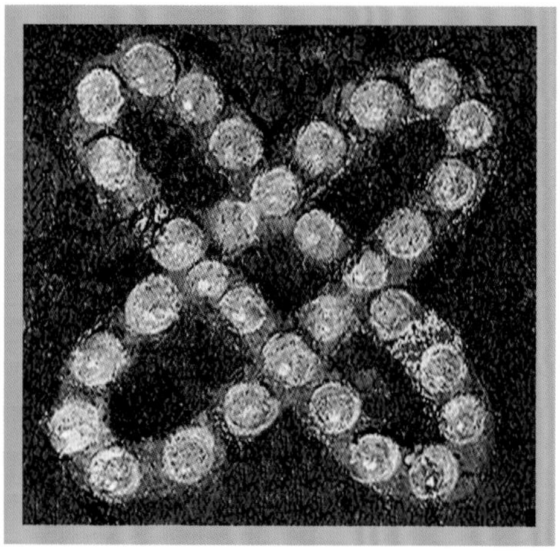

IMAGE 36
Solomon's Knot embroidered in pearls.
Graphic from a painting of Lady Jane Grey attributed to Master John.
England. Circa 1545 C.E.
computer graphic: Lois Rose Rose

"the essential knot in all its fashions"

In 1930 archaeologist Flinders Petrie published a collection of his drawings of thousands of design motifs. Of special relevance to this book are the symbols Petrie recorded under the heading of Double Links. They are variations of Solomon's Knot. During the thirteenth to the eighteenth century C.E. Jews were officially denied residence in England. Some English Jews fled North to Scotland and prospered there. Given that history, is the Knot symbol in Scottish Coats of Arms pictured by Petrie (e.g. Inverness and Glancar) for families with Jewish history, or is it an extension of Celtic art?

It would be wonderful to be able to ask Petrie what to make of the combination of Solomon's Knot on a fylfot, since it appears in his drawing of the Woodchester Coat of Arms, it is found in the original mosaic floor of the synagogue site upon which the Basilica Aquilea was later built, and it is prominent in the floor of a synagogue at the archaeological site at Sardis, Turkey. What, if any, is the relationship?

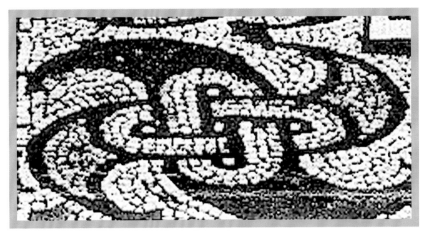

IMAGE 37
Detail of a synagogue floor at an archaeological site in Sardis, Turkey.

51

SEEING SOLOMON'S KNOT LOIS ROSE ROSE

VI – the process

Whether it's buttons...
or carpets...
or pie...

THINK

"Who's going to make it?
or bake it?
or buy?"

"buttons"

IMAGE 38
Clear plastic button with Solomon's Knot stamped on metal.
Mid-twentieth century C.E.

photography: Joel Lipton

All man made things carry information, but paints and fiber are perishable. Glass and metal trinkets are the better time travelers and they speak to the technology, artisans, customs, and beliefs of the culture and period in which they were made. The decorations on small objects may be simply that, decoration, with no other purpose than to please. This is especially true of contemporary ornament. Since the introduction of air travel, movies, television, copiers, and computers, design ideas travel quickly. Motifs are replicated at random, with ease. In addition, for many peoples, formerly strict dress codes for class, occasion, or group are now rare. Therefore, this modern plastic button demonstrates mid–twentieth century technology, but its metal Solomon's Knot probably bears no cultural or personal message.

This black glass button is from an earlier time, and this Solomon's Knot may have more significance. The button was made during the period when English Queen Victoria's mourning for her husband inspired a court led fashion for black dress and accessories. Many Jewish artisans were then working with glass and metal jewelry, and they were traditionally the button makers, as well. Coincidentally, during those years Solomon's Knot was being used on Jewish gravestones. So, the black glass button may have been made to adorn a garment inspired by Victorian royal black, or it may have been made to mark a commoner's loss, with both the maker and the mourner understanding the Knot's Jewish reference.

IMAGE 40
Stamped glass pendant with Solomon's Knot motif.
Circa fourth century C.E.
scan: Lois Rose Rose

Like buttons, this little glass pendant can focus attention on a very large matter, the question of choices. Whether authoring books, curating exhibitions, photographing sites, or purchasing acquisitions, one must make choices. Not everything everywhere can be collected or recorded. Those responsible for making the decisions about what will be shown or saved must rely on information and opportunity they have gained, and on a perception of what will be of interest to others.

Pendants such as this one were made in the Middle East during the late Roman and early Byzantine periods. The Israel Museum has published a book about the small objects in its Ancient Glass collection. There is an entire section devoted to pendants, many of them of stamped glass. Over fifty different designs are illustrated, but no Solomon's Knot is shown. It is hoped that the Museum's very able curatorial staff will take an interest in the Knot motif's significance.

IMAGE 41
Solomon's Knot in the Great Synagogue. Florence, Italy.

I note a similar situation with photographs of the Great Synagogue in Florence, Italy. I saw Solomon's Knots painted in the window arches of the upstairs Women's Section and a variation inlaid in the marble entrance floor. However, photographs of the Great Synagogue often appear in travel and architecture books, but the Solomon's Knots are not shown, presumably because their importance is not recognized.

So,
whether you are on a vacation or an expedition,
whether you find it near or far from home,

PLEASE

show and note
previously unnoticed Knots,
or noticed Knots not previously noted,
or formerly unknown, now known, Knots,
or known Knots not usually shown.

57

"carpets"

The symbols used in Central Asian textiles such as this carpet fragment are usually traditional, and their significance is generally well understood by the artisans who create them and the merchants who sell them. But Solomon's Knot is an exception, and it is not clear when it is considered a tribal or religious or regional design. Perhaps the Knot first circulated with Jewish traders or Jewish dyers of thread and later with waves of Moslems and Christians who traversed or settled in the area.

IMAGE 42
Solomon's Knots on a fragment of an antique Turkish kilim.
photography: Joel Lipton

58

"pie"

On a visit to the Camanche Dam construction site in Central California, I was treated to an apple pie that was heated in an oven officially used to dry soil samples. It was a delicious lesson in the versatility of technology. The difference between baking earth or food, firing ceramics, melting glass, or smelting metal is indeed just a matter of degree.

Since earliest times, techniques for generating, maintaining, and containing heat have linked many crafts. Ovens and kilns may have been cumbersome to move, but the know-how traveled well, and the path of Solomon's Knot becomes clearer when consideration is given to the trail of the technical skills that likely moved in tandem with the Knot.

For example, I photographed image 43 in the booth of an Iranian Moslem dealer at a London antiques

photography: Lois Rose Rose

IMAGE 43
Ceramic plate. Iran.

market. At first glance it is a piece of antique Islamic pottery. But, when one considers that Iran has always had and still has some Jewish population, and that this dish is similar in style and technique to a Passover Seder plate made in Spain just before the Inquisition, then a Jewish connection with the Knot is probable.

Image 44 is a plate that I purchased at a little shop in Velleko Turnova, Bulgaria. This ceramic, like image 43, has a Solomon's Knot at its center, and its glaze, colors, and other motifs are similar to the Persian plate with the possible Spanish–Jewish heritage. When I asked the shopkeeper, who was raised in an atheist political environment but had a shop filled with Christian/Moslem/Judaic based designs, whether he had a name or a tale about the motif on this particular plate, he said he just liked it.

He would probably be surprised to find that he may have sold a traditional ceremonial Seder plate, decorated with pigments, slips, and symbols that were taken to his region a thousand years before the design pleased him.

photography: Arnold B. Bristol

IMAGE 44
Ceramic plate. Bulgaria.

"who's going to make it"

A cross or an x?
The direction of
Solomon's Knot is a lot like love.
Keep silent, romance will remain,
speak your mind...you're a pain.
And the one you have adored
reveals all, and you are bored.
Things that are unclear
appeal year after year.
There's charm in ambiguity
designed so one can skew a tree
into a shadow, horse, or cat,
a could be this or could be that.
What you draw or say or mean
lives longest if it's in-between.

IMAGE 45
Damascene metal brooch. Toledo, Spain. Twentieth century C. E.

scan: Lois Rose Rose

"or bake it"

Across oceans, and centuries, tilemakers have baked enduring tiles decorated with Solomon's Knot. The tiles are used for fireplaces and fountains, walkways, and walls. The craftsmen's traditional techniques are still known; only the understanding of the Knot has been lost.

IMAGE 46
Solomon's Knot on glazed ceramic tile sidewalk inset.
Westwood, California. Twentieth century C.E.

photography: Lois Rose Rose

IMAGE 47
Solomon's Knot of grouted tile.
Patio, Honolulu Museum of Art. Hawaii. Twentieth century C.E.

photography: Lois Rose Rose

"or buy"

American heiress Doris Duke found two new loves on her first honeymoon in 1935. Aside from her husband, the twenty two year old bride was captivated by Middle Eastern architecture, then enchanted with Hawaii. While the marriage was not long lasting, her passion for exotic decor and natural beauty endured throughout her lifetime, and she managed to combine them in her Honolulu home, which she named *Shangri La*.

As a young and inexperienced collector with almost unlimited funds, she chose a team of advisors to help her build and decorate her personal paradise. Because she required her staff to find for her the best of the best, it followed that the staff commissioned artisans in a workshop in Rabat, Morocco to make for her the ceiling that I saw during my tour of *Shangri La* in 2004, a ceiling that was covered with the status symbol of royalty, Solomon's Knots of inlaid Mother-of-Pearl.

SEEING SOLOMON'S KNOT LOIS ROSE ROSE

VII—context

"WHO KNEW?" ABOUT THE KNOT. MANY TIMES "WHO KNEW?" IS SURELY KNOWN; CONTEXT MAKES IT CLEAR. THEN THE PRESENCE OF SOLOMON'S KNOT DEMONSTRATES THE CELEBRATION OF A PARTICULAR BELIEF SYSTEM OR ALLEGIANCE OR OCCUPATION.

Here are Solomon's Knots in a clearly Jewish context.

IMAGE 48
From a Pentateuch by Rabbi Nathan and Isaac ben Joshua.
951 C.E.

The Knot in a Moslem context

IMAGE 49
Title page of a Koran. Egypt. Early fourteenth century C.E.
graphic adaptation: Lois Rose Rose

THE PROMINENT PLACEMENT AND ELEGANT ARTISTRY OF THE KNOT
ON THE KORAN TITLE PAGE DEMONSTRATES THE SYMBOL'S SACRED
ALL—FAITH HISTORY.

The Knot in a Christian context

IMAGE 50

Solomon's Knots on the Epitaphios of carved olive wood from Jerusalem in the main sanctuary of Saint Sophia Greek Orthodox Cathedral in the "Byzantine District" of Los Angeles, California.

photography: Lois Rose Rose

CONSTRUCTION OF SAINT SOPHIA CATHEDRAL BEGAN IN 1948, AND THE CATHEDRAL WAS INAUGURATED IN 1952 C.E. DURING THE GOOD FRIDAY SERVICE THIS CARVED BALDACHINO, WHICH SYMBOLIZES THE HOLY SEPULCHER, IS LADEN WITH ICONS AND DECKED WITH FLOWERS. IT IS CARRIED IN A PROCESSION THROUGH THE CHURCH'S INTERIOR, THEN HELD HIGH FOR CONGREGANTS TO PASS BENEATH AS THEY EXIT.

⊠ WHY IS THE KNOT APPROPRIATE TO GRACE THE HONORED EPITAPHIOS?

⊠ HOW DOES THE KNOT'S USE SUGGEST THE EARLIEST HISTORY OF THE CHRISTIAN CHURCH?

67

Given time,
transmission,
and perhaps an agenda,
any translation will probably end a
little bit changed from when it started,
original meaning and current one parted.

Sometimes the terms for the Knot are fanciful. For example, a Solomon's Knot pendant shown in a mail order catalog is offered as a *Bride's Knot*. A similar piece in another catalog is called a *Serenity Knot*, another pendant with a gold Knot on jade is labeled an *Eternity Knot*, and still another version in another ad is called a *Friendship Knot*. A large metal knot ornament is advertised as a *Garden Knot;* and Solomon's Knots of any material or size often fall under the general term of *Celtic Knots*.

Conversely, many designs that are completely different interlaces are referred to by opportunists as Solomon's Knots. It is human nature.to call an object *Solomon's Something*. People desire to associate themselves or their products or progeny with those who seem to have it all. I Kings and II Chronicles provide a sort of biblical version of the television show *Life Styles of the Rich and Famous*. Solomon's Temple and his palace are described in lavish detail, providing a dream home for generations of believers of many faiths.

SOLOMON, AFTER THREE THOUSAND YEARS
OF IMAGE MAKING, HAS BECOME
The Maven with the Haven!

The wise King's flair has become the Italian Opera, the Elizabethan Theater, the Hollywood Spectacle of contemporary religious reference. And, in true Hollywood style, there is the hint of scandal that only adds to the legend. The reference in the Bible to King Solomon's one thousand women brings a more-than-macho, more-than-anybody, romantic aura to his image.

So Solomon has glamour, and his name is used to give whatever the namesake, however plain it may be, a touch of that appeal. For example, Solomon's Knot is the name of one of the basic knots used in the decorative fiber art form known as Macrame. In a very old book on Chinese Knotting, this same knot is called a Flat Knot. While the Macrame Solomon's Knot/Chinese Flat Knot does involve threads interlaced from opposite directions, neither the diagrams nor the finished product have the closed loops or links of the Solomon's Knot symbol seen in other crafts.

Since it already has a more accurate name, Flat Knot, why then the Macrame term Solomon's Knot? It's Human Nature and actually wise because both Solomon and his Knot are famous, so the term is useful, familiar, exotic, easy to remember.

HOORAY! FOR ALL THOSE MACRAME ARTISANS
WHO CHOOSE TO ENDOW THEIR FLAT KNOTS WITH
KING SOLOMON'S OOMPH.

69

IMAGE 51
Silhouetted Solomon's Knots
sculpted on the exterior of
the main synagogue in
Bucharest, Rumania.
Twentieth century C.E.

photography: Lois Rose Rose

IMAGE 52
Solomon's Knot is painted in repeat on the Rumanian
synagogue's interior walls. My outline indicates the
lines of a Knot with mitered tips. It interlaces with
stars, arabesques, and a classic Solomon's Knot.

SILHOUETTED OR INTRICATELY INTERLACED SOLOMON'S KNOTS SUCH
AS THE THE KNOTS EMBELLISHING THE MAIN SYNAGOGUE IN
BUCHAREST MAY BE DIFFICULT TO RECOGNIZE. CONSIDERING
CONTEXT, REMEMBERING THAT SOLOMON'S KNOT IS THE ALL—FAITH
SYMBOL WILL ENCOURAGE MORE CAREFUL OBSERVATION OF ANY
RELIGIOUS MEETING PLACE, VESTMENT, DOCUMENT OR ORNAMENT.

SOLOMON'S KNOT APPEARS IN ANCIENT MOSAICS.
THE CONTEXT IS SOMETIMES SECULAR, OFTEN SACRED.

Solomon's Knot in mosaic
so often proves Judaic,
one could suppose the tile art's name
and that of Moses are the same.

IMAGE 53, with detail.
Solomon's Knot in an ancient mosaic on display
at the Maritime Museum in Haifa, Israel.
photography: Lois Rose Rose

71

IMAGE 54
Solomon's Knot in the remnants of a mosaic floor
at a synagogue site in the old Roman port city of Ostia, Italy.
computer graphic adaptation: Lois Rose Rose

For thousands of years events have separated the Knot from its context. This has left many otherwise informed people puzzled that despite their active involvement in the study or the teaching of the arts or religion or history, the facts about Solomon's Knot are news to them. It is hard for them to understand how it could have just gotten lost or how they, eagle eyed collectors or scholars, could have missed this enduring, ubiquitous symbol.

During my lifetime, religious, racial, national, and gender identifications in the Western World have evolved from being used mainly as slurs in the generally anti-Semitic, racist atmosphere of pre-World War II to life threatening betrayals during the Holocaust to politically correct anonymity beginning in the nineteen sixties to the current period of open celebration of cultural variations. So, Solomon's Knot has played peek-a-boo with Western scholars; deliberately invisible or incidentally lost in the disconnects of Jewish expulsions, hidden from the understanding of early exploiters or explorers with their White European attitude in Black Africa, assimilated beyond recognition into the elaborations of Celtic/Christian art.

72

On the coast of Israel I found a Solomon's Knot with a clear shape and an unclear context. It was in the mosaic floor of what was probably a walled stall or shop in Caesarea, the region's capital city during the Roman period. Because it was in an apparent market area, it seems unlikely that this was a religious sanctuary. The Knot has been shown to represent metal work. Could this have been the shop of a metalsmith? Too impractical, I think. Many modern day bazaars have a stall where currency can be changed. Could some sort of financial service have been provided here? Or, since the Knot is one of several interlaced motifs in the beautifully crafted floor, the type of design combination that appears in earlier Roman period mosaics, perhaps this floor was formerly part of non-commercial space that was, centuries later, divided into a marketplace.

Why is Solomon's Knot there?
Why is Solomon's Knot ever where it is?

Convergent or parallel,
on trajectory or carousel?
Is this Knot a loop or link?
One we create or learn to think?
Are we moving it in space?
Finding it as we search for grace?
Must every generation tell
about the Knot, each place we dwell?

73

SEEING SOLOMON'S KNOT LOIS ROSE ROSE

VIII—more to explore

MY OWN AND COLLEAGUE'S RESEARCH HAS REVEALED MANY KNOTS
WHOSE SIGNIFICANCE IS NOT YET KNOWN. MORE INVESTIGATION IS
NEEDED, SO, I EXTEND THIS INVITATION TO EACH OF YOU...

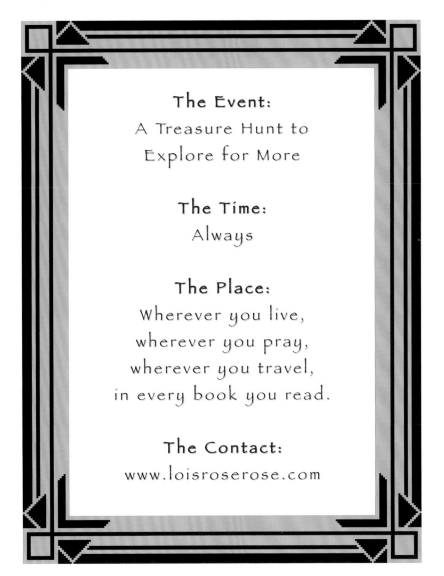

The Event:
A Treasure Hunt to
Explore for More

The Time:
Always

The Place:
Wherever you live,
wherever you pray,
wherever you travel,
in every book you read.

The Contact:
www.loisroserose.com

WHAT FOLLOWS IS A SAMPLING OF KNOTS TO TEMPT YOU. THEY ARE
JUST WAITING TO BE EXPLORED, SHARED, AND COMPARED. JOIN THE
FUN, (IT REALLY IS FUN) AND TAKE THIS STUDY FURTHER.

THE RELATIVELY SAFE PRESENT IS THE TIME, PERHAPS THE LAST, THE ONLY TIME, TO RETRIEVE THE INFORMATION, ALL THE INFORMATION, THAT WAS DESPERATELY HIDDEN, INADVERTENTLY LOST, OR CARELESSLY GARBLED IN THE PAST. HERE'S HOW...

Tell the place and origins
of artifacts and artisans,
ignoring current Middle Eastern
biased political partisans.
Be specific and complete
concerning ways the cultures grew,
naming all the peoples,
be they Hittite, Greek, or Jew.
Don't be afraid to use the words
that best describe the site,
the people and traditions,
even when they're Israelite.
If you treat all facts objectively,
you will speak the truth effectively...
just saying
"from the Levant"
you can't.

• in Uzbekistan, you bet you can...

find a Knot on a cot!

IMAGE 55
Solomon's Knot embroidered on a cotton bedding cover.
Uzbekistan. 1990s C.E.

scan: Lois Rose Rose

• make inquiry in Italy

photography: Lois Rose Rose

IMAGE 56

Solomon's Knot carved in stone. Palazzo Nuovo, a Capitoline Museum. Rome, Italy. There was no citation and no one to ask when I saw this at the museum.

ASK WHAT? WHERE? WHEN? WHO MADE IT?

and

• the next time you are in Libya deliberate about...

THE ANCIENT RUINS AT GERMA IN THE FEZZAN, WHICH HAVE MANY MOSAIC SOLOMON'S KNOTS. ACCORDING TO THE LIBYAN GOVERNMENT, ROMAN RUINS LIKE THOSE OF LEPTIS MAGNA REMIND US THAT MERCHANTS AND ARTISANS FROM MANY PARTS OF THE ROMAN WORLD ESTABLISHED THEMSELVES IN NORTH AFRICA, AND THAT UNDER THE PTOLEMIES, CYRENAICA HAD BECOME THE HOME OF A LARGE JEWISH COMMUNITY WHICH INCREASED BY TENS OF THOUSANDS WHEN JEWS WERE DEPORTED THERE AFTER THE FAILURE OF THE REBELLION AGAINST ROMAN RULE IN PALESTINE, AND THE DESTRUCTION OF JERUSALEM IN B.C.E. 70. PERHAPS YOUR DELIBERATIONS WILL REVEAL SPECIFICALLY WHO DESIGNED, WHO CRAFTED, WHO WALKED UPON, WHO WORSHIPED LIBYA'S KNOT LADEN MOSAICS.

IMAGE 57

Detail from a mosaic floor. Sabatha. Libya.

IMAGE 58
From a bronze brooch.
Kakuzenu Miklas Kains, Latvia.
Tenth to twelfth century C.E.

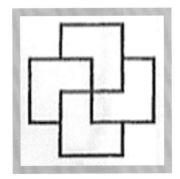

IMAGE 59
Potters mark from a ceramic vessel.
Kokonese, Latvia.
Tenth to twelfth century C.E.

- learn a lot via Latvia

- tsee the Knot on Russian Tsars

- czeck out old Czech Chanukah lamps

- polish up on Jewish tombstones in Poland

- strain your brain in Spain

WHEN YOU FIND SOLOMON'S KNOT IN A SYNAGOGUE FLOOR, CIRCA FOURTH CENTURY C.E. IN ELCHE, SPAIN. ELCHE IS A CITY IN SOUTHEAST SPAIN. AN ANCIENT ROMAN COLONY, IT WAS HELD BY THE MOORS FROM THE EIGHTH TO THE THIRTEENTH CENTURIES C.E.

- pore over porcelain in Galicia...

IMAGE 60
Solomon's Knot on a porcelain box. On the side of the box is written "Galicia Celca", a reference to a Celtic presence in Galicia that began in the Middle Ages when a small group of Celts settled in the region.

scans: Lois Rose Rose

79

• be a big name hunter in Africa

IMAGE 61
Adinkra Cloth. Sacred symbols hand stamped on woven cotton.
Africa. Twentieth century C.E.

On a sword, on a gourd,
on a textile adored,
Solomon's Knot
signs an African Lord.

IMAGE 62
Head rest with tooled Solomon's Knots, Zaire.
The head rest's shape was also used
as a shape for coins in the former Belgian Congo.
photography: Lois Rose Rose

SOLOMON'S KNOTS APPEAR ON BEADED THRONES, CARVED IVORY
SWORDS, CALABASH ART, DOOR PANELS, SECRET SACRED PRINTS
AND ROYAL HEAD RESTS. EACH SYMBOL IS A MEANINGFUL PERSONAL
SELECTION. WHO WILL DISCOVER WHAT GUIDED EACH AFRICAN
DIGNITARY'S INDIVIDUAL CHOICE?

• in Israel where the Knot is real...

VISIT ZIPPORI NATIONAL PARK. THERE THE SOLOMON'S KNOTS ARE IN A ROMAN PERIOD SYNAGOGUE SITE WITHIN THE ISRAELI PARK. PERHAPS YOU WILL BE THE ONE TO TELL WHAT THESE MOSAIC KNOTS MEANT TO THE PEOPLE WHO PRAYED AND MADE OFFERINGS AT THEIR TEMPLE IN ZIPPORI.

IMAGE 63
Solomon's Knot on a fylfot.

IMAGE 64
Solomon's Knot of graduated links.

IMAGE 65
Solomon's Knot of closed curves.

81

• mount a search in Canada, enlist the Army

IMAGE 66
Solomon's Knot enameled on a letter opener.
Solomon's Knots in gold. Military collar decorations.
Army Logistics/Logistique Canada.
photography: Joel Lipton

NEW WORLD MILITARY BADGES USE OLD WORLD HERALDIC
IMAGERY, SOMETIMES MIXED WITH INDIAN SYMBOLS.
SOLOMON'S KNOT APPEARS IN HISTORIC BRITISH AND
FRENCH DESIGNS AND IN INDIAN ICONOGRAPHY. COULD
THE LOGIC OF THE KNOT AS THE LOGISTICS EMBLEM BE ITS
IMPLICATIONS OF INTEGRATING FROM ALL DIRECTIONS?

82

• delve deeply in the South

IMAGE *67*
The Knot stamped on a pottery vessel.
Fifteenth century C.E. Mound Building Civilization. USA.

IN CHATHAM COUNTY, GEORGIA, YOU MIGHT WANT TO ASK ABOUT THE IRENE MOUND SITE. POTTERY EXCAVATED AT THAT SITE SHOWS THAT FOR A PERIOD OF ABOUT TWO HUNDRED YEARS THE KNOT WAS STAMPED ON MANY CLAY VESSELS. PERHAPS THE REFINED DESIGN AND LIMITED DURATION OF THE KNOT'S USE COULD REVEAL MORE ABOUT THE TRADE PATTERNS AND PRACTICES OF THE IRENE COMMUNITY, INCLUDING MESO AMERICAN INFLUENCE FORESHADOWED BY THE KNOT'S PRESENCE ON A CERAMIC EFFIGY OF THE NICOYA PEOPLE OF GUANCASTE, COSTA RICA, EARLY IN THE FIRST MILLENNIUM C.E.

• examine the prospects in the West

MINE FOR NUGGETS OF INFORMATION ABOUT THE HUGE SOLOMON'S KNOT ON THE SHIELD CARRIED BY A PARTICIPANT IN A PIONEER AWARDS CEREMONY GIVEN BY LOS DESCENDIENTES DEL PRESIDIO DURING THE FIESTA DE SAN AGUSTIN IN ARIZONA IN 1995.

ROUND UP THE REASON A MODERN HOPI/LAGUNA ARTISAN INCORPORATES THE KNOT IN A JEWEL STUDDED SILVER BREASTPLATE.

IMAGE 68
Solomon's Knot on a Plains Indian Medicine Bag.
Buckskin with medallions of beadwork applied on both sides of bag.
The leather is threaded with glass beads.
North America. 1920 C.E.
photography: Joel Lipton

IX—how it *really* began

CONJURERS USE SOLOMON'S KNOT TO CAST SPELLS.

GEOMANCERS FORECAST THE FUTURE WITH SOLOMON'S KNOT.

SOLOMON'S KNOTS APPEAR ON DIVINATION BOARDS.

SOLOMON'S KNOT IS
THE LOGO WITH THE MOJO!

IT HAS BEEN A FORCE IN MY LIFE FOR A VERY LONG TIME...

Did you ever wonder
if you're under
a spell?
I say
the best way
to tell
is by what you crave
and what you save
and what you would not sell.
Your memory's voice is
commanding your choices,
an enchantment no reason can quell.

IMAGE 69
Solomon's Knot detail from the inlaid wood ceiling of
the Main Reading Room in Powell Library.
University of California, Los Angeles.
Powell Library was originally built circa 1928 C.E.

Experience has shown me that we all seek out, time and time again, the images that remind us of our dearest moments. I call it my *Little Glass Lamp Theory* because I find that many of the things that I create or enjoy have colors and a pattern that I associate with a little glass lamp that shone on loving, cozy childhood visits to my grandparents' home.

My search for Solomon's Knot **seemed** to begin in my silk screen studio about 1980. In 2002 I learned its earlier origin. While revisiting the Powell Library at UCLA, I was astonished to find that the Knot had in fact cast its spell on me years before, when, as a student, I happily flirted, dozed, and occasionally studied beneath the ceiling of the lovely Main Reading Room, a ceiling lined with what I now recognize as Solomon's Knots.

THAT'S HOW THE SEARCH *REALLY* BEGAN!

photography: Dirk Wales

IMAGE 70
The author, under a spell.

SEEING SOLOMON'S KNOT LOIS ROSE ROSE

BEWARE!
YOU ARE ENTERING A BIBLIOGRAPHY

IMAGE 71
Yoruba crown.with glass beadwork. Africa. Early twentieth century C.E.
photography: Joel Lipton

PRESERVATION is a matter of
chance,
preparation,
and climate.

OBSERVATION may be a matter of
chance,
preparation,
and political climate.

INTERPRETATION could be a matter of
chance,
lack of preparation,
or political opportunity.

So,
when searching and researching,
it is necessary to ask
whether the answers you find show
sense,
sensitivity,
or censorship because

as this clued in
researcher insights it,
it matters who finds it;
it matters who writes it.
And where!
And when!

books, listed by title

Africa Adorned
Angela Fisher
Harry N. Abrams, Inc., Publishers, New York.
1984
ISBN 0-8109-1823-4

pps. 96, 98 In the text and magnificent photographs of *Africa Adorned,* the author's notes on **p.96** regarding a Yoruba *Ade,* the beaded crown worn by Obas who claim to be descendants of the mythical first king of Ife, describe the birds and human images represented in the beadwork. She does not mention the four *imbolos,* the *Solomon's Knots,* clearly shown in the photograph on **p.98. I suggest that these symbols, prominent on many Yoruba crowns, refer to the links of the iron chain provided to first man by Odun.**

pps. 292-293 Angela Fisher notes, with her photograph of assorted Ethiopian neck crosses, that they have been worn as symbols of faith for 1600 years. There are regional versions of Christian crosses, and some with a star motif are attributed to a small group of Jewish settlers. She also describes the interlaces that appear on some of the pendants as symbols of Eternity, and probably of Celtic origin.

My research shows that there is an even longer and richer history to these ornaments.

African Ark
Carol Beckwith, Angela Fisher
Harry N. Abrams, Inc.
New York
1990
ISBN 0-8109-1902-8

p. 51 Drawing of King Solomon and the Queen of Sheba in the Act of Conception
Text of **chapter 2**

African Art, Definition, Forms and Styles
Edited by R.O. Rom Kalilu
Ladoke Akintola University of Technology, Ogbomoso
Nigeria
1992

p.34 The Knot interlace carved on a gourd. Gourd carving is a centuries old tradition of the Yoruba People that is in danger of becoming a lost art.

1

African Art and Leadership

Edited by Douglas Fraser and Herbert M. Cole
University of Wisconsin Press
Madison. Milwaukee and London
1972
p. 85 Cole, Ibo Art and Authority.
pps. 143-144 Fraser, Symbols of Ashanti Kingship
re: a King's ceremonial stool. Fraser remarks on the personal choices of various African leaders. **p,209, p. 215, p. 283, p.290, p.318** Fraser asserts that more attention should be paid to the significance of the Knot motif.

African Kings

Daniel Laine
Ten Speed Press
Berkeley, Toronto
Published 1991
ISBN: 1-58008-272-6
p.63 Two Nigerian chiefs, Oba Oyebade Lipede, Alake of Abeokuta, wear garments with embroidered *Solomon's Knots* (*imbolos*).

African Textiles

Christopher Spring
Crescent Books
New York
1989
ISBN 0-517-688077
plate 11 Embroidered man's pants with Solomon's Knot which Spring labels an *Islamic Knot*. Hausa People, Northern Nigeria.

African Textiles and Decorative Arts

Roy Sieber
The Museum of Modern Art
New York
1972
ISBN: 0-87070-227-0
p.38 Hausa embroidery example.
p.159 Kaisi velvet reference.

American Indian Design & Decoration

(formerly titled Art of the Americas)
Le Roy H. Appleton

Dover Publications, Inc.
New York
Published 1950, 1971
ISBN: 0-486-22704-9
p.182 The Forest and the Rivers, Southern Appalachian
Solomon's Knot.

Ancient Cities of the Indus Valley Civilization
Jonathan Mark Kenoyer
American Institute of Pakistan Studies
Oxford University Press
United Kingdom
1998
ISBN 0 19 577940 1
p.107 Kenoyer's thoughts on abstract symbols.

Ancient Glass in the Israel Museum
Maud Spear
The Israel Museum
Jerusalem
2001
ISBN:965 278260 2

Ancient Mosaics
Roger Ling
Princeton University Press
New York
1998
ISBN:0-691-00404-8
p.17 example of Solomon's Knots used as a decorative motif in a non-religious, non-political third century C.E. European setting.
p.53 example of the Knot in an Antioch mosaic pavement.
The focus of this book seems to be entirely on residential uses of mosaics in the Greek and Roman periods. Lovely photographs and an odd text concentrating on author Ling's modern critique of ancient art work. In my opinion, his opinion makes his text generally pointless. Art criticism, where it is art history that is wanted, is of no value.

Archaologische mitteilungen aus Iran und Turan
Deutsches archaologisches institut
Band 30

Berlin, Germany
1998

Art and History of Florence
Casa Editrice Bonechi
Florence
1991
p. 144 Israelite Temple

The Art of African Textiles
Duncan Clarke
Thunder Bay Press
San Diego, California
1997
ISBN: 1-57145-132-3
p. 18 A Yoruba Chief displays his Aso Ake Robe, Nigeria, 1960.
pps. 54-55 Cut pile embroidered raffia panel. Kuba Kingdom, Kasai Region, Zaire. **p. 61** Details of men's raffia applique dance skirt, Kuba Kingdom, Kasai Region, Zaire, show clearly the prototype for the details that are included with the Knots in the modern scarf shown with the traditional Kuba cloth in Seeing Solomon's Knot. **p.98** Photograph of a master weaver with *imbolos*, Solomon's Knots embroidered on his robe, Oyo, 1996. **An example of the Knot worn by a commoner who has status perhaps by virtue of his craftsmanship and wealth, rather than his genealogy or political status.**

The Art of Macrame
Joan Fisher
The Hamlyn Publishing Group
London
1972
ISBN: 0-600-360466
p.31 Reference to Solomon's Knot **p.37** Reference to Solomon's Bar.

The Arts of Africa
Rene S. Wassing
Thames and Hudson
London
1970
500 23127 3

4

pps. 31-32, 254 catalog 72 Hausa men's robe, and **catalog 72** Adinkra cloth.

Wassing's description of the Hamitic People may be an important clue to the path of the Knot.

Art Royal Kuba

Coronet, Sipiel
Milan
1982
In French, a discussion of the *imbolo.*

The Atlas of Rugs & Carpets

Edited by David Black
Tiger Books International
London
1996
ISBN: 1-85501-500-5
p. 206 The Wheel carpet.

Back to the Sources

Edited by Barry Holtz
Summit Books
New York
1984
p. 321 Ten definitions of the Shechinah, as derived from the Kabbalah, showing that the name of the Divine Presence may be Anglicized several ways. **The Bride, the Shechinah invites or indicates G-d's presence. Could Solomon's Knot mean a Shechinah?**

Beads Body and Soul

Authors: Henry John Drewal and John Mason
UCLA Fowler Museum of Cultural History
Los Angeles
1998
ISBN: 0-930741-63-3 soft cover
I had originally planned to request permission from the Fowler Museum to use the catalog images that illustrated Solomon's Knot in the Yoruba culture. However, when I realized how many images there were that showed the Knot, it seemed better to simply give specific references of outstanding examples, rather than seek to reprint such a large portion of their beautiful catalog.

The *Solomon's Knots* are simply referred to as decorative interlaces, in spite of the fact that they are often the dominant motifs. Only when the *Knot* is the only motif are comments made. In those cases, while no African title is offered, the authors speculate on p.250 and p.270 that the interlace may represent the idea of an unending cycle of life, death, departure, and return. This seems consistent with other interpretations that refer to the *Knot* as eternal. **p. 41** Beaded cushion of the Olota of Ota with multiple *Solomon's Knots*. Awori-Yoruba. **p.57 figure 50** Beaded decorations for talking drums, mother drum (lead drum), Yoruba. **p.66 fig 68a** Beaded crown with bead veil, Yoruba. **p.237 cat.44** Yoruba beadwork for King Owa, 1929. **p.263 cat.68** Beaded dance panel. **p.271 cat.73** Egungun ensemble with beaded panel descending from headdress.

The Book of Divination
Ann Fiery
Chronicle Books
San Francisco
1999
ISBN: 0-8118-2641-4
pps.161-168 Geomancy

Born in Blood
The Lost Secrets of Freemasonry
John J. Robinson
M. Evans & Company
New York
1989
ISBN: 0-87131-602-1
pps. 208, 241-242, 278-279 Because the symbolism of Solomon's Temple is used so extensively in Masonic ritual, a study of *Solomon's Knot* must address that issue. Robinson's exploration of the origins and meanings of Masonic iconography is comprehensive, making it a useful general reference for this subject, but I found no secrets revealed about the *Knot*.

Brewer's Dictionary of Phrase and Fable, 14th Edition
Ivor H. Evans
Harper & Row

New York

1989

pps. 198, 938, 1036 References to legends about King Solomon.

The Bronze Age Civilization of Central Asia

Recent Soviet Discoveries

M.E. Sharpe, Inc.

Armonk, New York

1981

p.233 From the Gonur 1 settlement. **figure 4 Reference is made to a seal with depiction of dragons that has direct parallels to the depiction of intertwined snakes on a cult slab from Elam. Comment is made that one must consider that the drawing itself has magical significance, being without an end or a beginning, possibly symbolizing the concept of longevity or immortality.**

p. 248 Note is made that another concept related to the phallic shaped snake is sexuality, related to the idea of fertility.

Buttons

Diana Epstein, Millecent Safro

Harry N. Abrams, Inc., Publishers

New York

1991

ISBN: 0-8109-3113-3

p.86 By the 1880s jet buttons had been surpassed in popularity by black glass buttons which were made in the then predominant glass centers, Venice, Bohemia, and Austria. **This raises the question of whether black glass buttons with a** *Solomon's Knot* **motif were intended as a general sign of Eternity, or if the artisans who made them, many of whom were Jewish, recognized this as the symbol that was frequently used on Jewish tombstones in parts of Europe, including Venice.**

Calabash, Oyo

Stratliches Museum fur Vocker Kunde

Munich, Germany

19th century

p.15 *Solomon's Knot* represents Aye and Orun of the Cosmos.

1950

The Cathedral of Sienna

Aldo Lusini
Sienna, Italy
1950
pps. 20-21 The choir stall, carved 1363 to 1425. **plate 49** Photo of stalls with variations of *Solomon's Knot*.

Celtic Art, The Methods of Construction

George Bain
Dover Publications, Inc.
New York
1951, 1973
ISBN: 0486-22923-8
pps. 27, 59, 71, 87 Examples and history of *Solomon's Knot* with many elaborations.

Chinese Knotting

Lydia Chen
Echo Publishing Company, Ltd
Taipei, Taiwan, Republic of China
1981
ISBN: 0-8048-1389-2
p.58

Christie's Catalog

The Erlenmeyer Collection
of Ancient Near Eastern Stamp Seals and Amulets
Christie, Manson & Woods Ltd.
London, England
Auction June 6, 1989
Lot 185 Cruciform interlace carved stone seal, Ubaid, circa 4500 B.C.E.

Christie's Catalog

Antiquities
June 11, 2003
New York
2003
p.196 item 223 A Roman Marble Mosaic Panel, circa 2nd-3rd Century C.E. cited as a Solomon knot circle.

Chronicle of the Old Testament Kings
John Rogerson
Thames and Hudson
New York
1999
ISBN: 0-500-05095-3
Interesting for the candid observations regarding the difficulty of obtaining accurate ancient data from biblical texts.

The Concise Alcalay Dictionary English/Hebrew
Reuben Alcalay
Printed in Israel
1995

A Concise History of Irish Art
Bruce Arnold
Frederick A. Praeger, Publishers
New York, Washington
1968
Library of Congress Catalog Number 68-54497
pps. 11, 20-21, 27, 43, 52 Traces progress of interlace motifs from the East to Ireland.

The Da Vinci Code
Dan Brown
Doubleday
New York
2003
ISBN: 0-385-50420-9
Fiction that offers an interesting take on the significance that ancient symbols may acquire, e.g. **pps. 145, 309, 445- 446.**

Decorative Patterns of the Ancient World
Flinders Petrie
Bracken Books
London
1930, 1995
ISBN: 1-85891-278-4
plate Twist: Double Links, **plate** Shields: Roman, Gallic, Scythian, **plate**: Band of Balls, **plate**: Cross Emblems, 1400 to Roman Age, **plate**: Pavement Mosaics l:l angle.

Decorative Tiles Throughout the Ages

Hanns Van Lemmen
Moyer Bell
Rhode Island
1997
ISBN: 1-55921-161-X

p.31 plate 10 *Solomon's Knot* tile, France, 1870.
p.43 plate 16 *Solomon's Knot* tile, England, 1880.

The Dictionary of Needlework

S. F. A. Caulfield & B. C. Saward
Blankton Hall Ltd, London
Published 1989 reprinted from the second edition of 1885
ISBN: 0-907854-10-9

pps. 332, 453 Diagram and definition of *Solomon's Knot* in macrame.

Dictionary of Symbols

Carl G. Liungman
Publisher
W.W. Norton & Company
New York, London
!991
ISBN: 0-393-31236-4

pps. 269-270 Drawings and interpretations of *Solomon's Knot* as an ideogram for the atom.

Dictionary of Symbolism

Hans Biedermann, translated by James Hulbert
Facts on File
New York, Oxford
1989
ISBN: 0-8160-2593-2

pps. 63-64, 197-199, 313-314 Study of folkloric beliefs about Chains and Knots.

Die Kunst der Antiker Synagoge

Baruch Kaneal
Ner-Tamid-Verlac
Munchen, Frankfurt

figure 61 Mosaic floor at Beth Alpha. **figure 70** Carpet, Aegina Synagogue.

DK Illustrated Oxford Dictionary
DK Publishing, Inc.
London
Oxford University Press
Oxford
1998
ISBN: 0-7894-3557-8
p.448 *knop/nop/ n. 1 a knob, esp. ornamental. 2 an ornamental loop or tuft in yarn.*

Doris Duke's Shangri La
Sharon Littlefield
Honolulu Academy of Arts
Doris Duke Foundation for Islamic Arts
2002
ISBN: 0-937426-57-1
p.18 *Solomon's Knots* in living room ceiling. **p.34** Ceiling in progress in a workshop in Rabat, Morocco, 1938.

The Eighth Day
The Hidden History of the Jewish Contribution to Civilization
Samuel Kurinsky
Jason Aronson, Inc.
New Jersey, London
1994
ISBN:0-87667-587-4
p.281 *Solomon's Knots* in mosaic floors, illustrations and text.

Elam
Pierre Amiet
Centre National de la Recherche Scientifique
Archee Editeur
1966
L'Epoque Sumero-Elamite Ancienne
p.173 figure 124, Louvre, Sr 2724 Relief cultuel.

Fodor's Exploring Israel
Andrew Sanger
Fodor's Travel Productions, Inc.
New York, Washington
1996
ISBN: 0-679-03009-3
p. 118

Gifted Hands, Jewish Artisans, Ornament and Beads

Lois Rose Rose
Los Angeles
1998
ISBN 0-9668645-0-6
A view of the craftsmen who carried the crafts that carried the Knot.

The Glassmakers, An Odyssey of the Jews

Samuel Kurinsky
Hippocrene Books
New York
1991
ISBN: 0-87052-901-3
An important resource for evaluating and re-evaluating historical evidence.

Graven Images, Graphic Motifs of the Jewish Gravestone

Arnold Schwartzman
Harry N. Abrams, Inc. Publishers
New York
1993
ISBN: 0-8109-3377-2
front cover emboss, **frontispiece** drawing of Solomon's Knot
p. 58 A photo of Solomon's Knot on a Jewish tombstone.

A Guide to the Archaeology and History of County Kerry

Kerry County Museum
Tralee Urban District Council
London
1992
The Celts, 500 B.C.E.- 500 C.E.

A Handbook of Celtic Ornament

John G. Merne
Dover Publications, Inc.
Mineola, New York
2002 Edition, originally published 1931

ISBN 0-486-41968-6

p. 7 Introduction. *Solomon's Knot* diagrams **p. 81 plate 36
figures A1, A6, B1, B2, B3, C1, C2, p. 85 plate 38 G1, H4, J1, J2,
P. 93 plate 42, figures 6, 7, 8, 9, 10**.

Hebrew Illuminated Manuscripts

Bezalel Narkiss
Forward by Cecil Roth
Encyclopedia Judaica, Jerusalem
Leon Amiel Publisher, New York
1969, 1974
ISBN: 8148-0593-0

pps. 48-49 plate 4 Yemenite Pentateuch. **pps. 136-137 plate 48**
Vatican Arba'ah Turim.

The History of Beads

Lois Sherr Dubin
Harry N. Abrams, Inc., Publishers
New York
1987
ISBN: 0-8109-0736-4

p.100 figure 91 The Knot on a nineteenth century Venetian
made glass bead traded in West Africa.

The Holy Bible

King James Version
Illuminated Family Edition
Thunder Bay Press
San Diego, California
Compilation © 2000 by Lionheart Books, Ltd.
ISBN: 1-57145-282-6

The Holy Scriptures, According to the Masoretic Text

The Jewish Publication Society of America
Philadelphia
5708-1948 (22nd impression)
Original copyright 1917

Ife: Origins of Art and Civilization

Henry John Drewal and John Pembarton III
Center for African Art in association with Henry N. Abrams Inc.
New York
1989

p. 38 Beads. **pps. 44-75** Nine Centuries of African Art. **p. 108** Ceremonial Sword. **p. 124** Concerning the use of the interlace on Yoruba objects associated with leaders, rulers and priests, Drewal writes that the interlace filtered South from the Hausa Sokoto Califate, and is so readily accepted and dispersed that it must evoke a deep, indigenous mental icon, especially since it appears on the most sacred forms. He also posits that it reflects fundamental Yoruba philosophical concepts about competing forces in the cosmos. **Drewal's comments do justice the the profound significance of the Knot.**

Indian Art of the Americas

Frederick J. Dockstader
Museum of American Indian
Heye Foundation
New York
1973
Library of Congress Catalog Number 73-89979
p. 111 Nicoya clay figurine with Knot incised.

Irene Mound Site

Chatham County, Georgia USA
Joseph Caldwell and Catherine McCann
University of Georgia Press
Athens, Georgia USA
1941
figure 20 Irene Fylfot Stamped. Image of the classic Knot stamped on clay pottery, with three other variations of the symbol. **An especially interesting progression.**

Irish Archaeology

Edited by Michael Ryan
Town House and Country House
Dublin
1991, 1997
ISBN: 0-946172-33-1
pps. 12-16 Michael Ryan brilliantly defines the problems facing archaeologists.
I would add my own observations, based on the many opportunities I had to understand my late husband and his associates, field engineers and geologists, keeping their professional objectivity no matter what personal

14

discomfort, danger or sacrifice was encountered in gathering particular information. It seemed to me that there was the constant threat of becoming committed to a theory simply because the data for it was so very hard to gather. I salute the field researchers in every discipline, who daily, valiantly manage to keep their perspective. p. 154-155.

Israel
Neil Tilbury
Lonely Planet Publications
Hawthorn, Australia
1992
ISBN: 0-86442-128-1
pps. 290-292 Caesarea. This is a handy, short reference to a subject that has been written about long and often.

Japanese Crests
Electronic Clip Art
Dover Publications
New York
ISBN: 0-486-99561-5
2003
p. 1 Knot designs **004, 007.**

Jewish Art
Grace Cohen Grossman
Encyclopedia Judaica, Jerusalem
Leon Amiel Publisher, New York
1995
ISBN: 0-88363-361-2
p. 58 *Vatican Arba'ah Turim,* Mantua, 1435 C.E. Solomon's Knot at top center of border. **p. 216** Passover Plate, Spain c.1480 C.E. **p.230** Hanukkah lamp, italy, fourteenth century, C.E. with Solomon's Knot outline.

Jewish Art
Edited by Cecil Roth
McGraw Hill Book Company, Inc.
New York•Toronto•London
1961
Mosaic floor in the synagogue El-Hammach, Transjordan.
Ernst Cohn-Weiner, afterword by Hannelore Kunzl

Jewish Art, Its History from the Beginning to the Present Day

Berlin 1929
Translation by Anthea Bell
Pilkington Press, Yelvertoft Manor, Northamptonshire
English Reprint 2001
ISBN: 1 899044 272

p. 39 Text. **p. 118** **figures 74, 75** Spanish Pentateuch. **p. 131** **figure 86. p. 147** **figure 95. p. 148 figure 145** Pentateuchs.

Jewish Carpets

Anton Felton
Antique Collectors' Club Ltd.
Woodbridge, Suffolk, U.K.
1997
ISBN: 1-85149-259-3

pps. 57-60 **Particularly insightful analysis of the legends and lore surrounding symbols used in the textile arts. Also, pictured from the Felton collection, a Kashan carpet from the 1850s depicting King Solomon and the Queen of Sheba seated on his fabled throne.**

Jewish Ceremonial Art

Abram Kanof
Harry N. Abrams inc., Publishers
New York
1969, 1974
ISBN: 8109-2199-5

p. 62 figure 38 Solomon's Knots, small and unnoted in tilework at the Alhambra, Spain. **p. 165** Hanukkah lamp with Solomon's Knot outline.

Jewish Symbols in the Greco-Roman Period

Volume Three
Bollingen Series xxxvii
Pantheon Books
figures 627, 631, 639, 642, 649, 650 Images of Solomon's Knot in mosaic floors at various sites.

The Jewish Word Book

Sidney Jacobs
Jonathan David Publishers
New York, Oxford

1982
ISBN: 0-0-671-07538-1
pps. 264-265 Definition and alternate spellings of *Schechinuh, The Divine Presence.*

Jews and Synagogues
Venice, Florence, Rome, Leghorn
Umberto Fortis
Stirti Edizioni
Venezia
1973
Library of Congress Catalog Card Number 72-93070
pps. 19, 38, 86, 102.

Jordan
Annual of the Department of Antiquities
1984
p. 357 figure 6.

Judaism in Stone
The Archaeology of Ancient Synagogues
Herschel Shanks
Biblical Archaeology Society
New York/Washington D,C.
1979
ISBN 0-06-0672188
p. 116 Hammeth Gader, a reconstruction of a mosaic carpet with Solomon's Knots.

Knots & Splices
Percy W. Blandford
Arco Publishing Company, Inc.
New York
1976
ISBN: 0-668-01331-1
p. 9 General history of knots.

Larousse Encyclopedia of Byzantine and Medieval Art
Edited by Rene Huyghe
Prometheus Press
New York
1958, 1963
Library of Congress Catalog Card Number 63-12755
p. 87 Islamic art's debt to its predecessors. **374 figure 953**

17

Solomon's Knot over a decorative window in the 15th century Bourges home of Jacques Couer, treasurer to King Charles VII. Since the most successful financial advisors at that time were often the "*Court Jews*", perhaps that symbol carried with it a religious connotation, or it may have been used to denote the fact that the owner dealt in money or in precious metal.

The Legacy of Ghengis Kahn

Metropolitan Museum of Art
Edited by Linda Kamaroff and Stefano Carboni
Yale University Press
New Haven and London
frontispiece and **p. 164 figure 192** Shah Zai Enthroned. Rows of *Solomon's Knots* across the bottom portion of a court painting. **p. 41** Comments on Rashid al-Din, a Jewish convert to Islam, and his *Compendium of Chronicles* with its numerous references to the Jewish presence in the Mongol Empire, may provide a clue as to one particular, influential, knowledgeable tastemaker who brought a Biblical Jewish King's symbol onto the Mongol throne.

The Living Nach

Early Prophets
A New Translation Based on Traditional Jewish Sources
The Living Torah Series
Yaakov Elman
Moznaim Publishing Corporation
New York/Jerusalem
5754-1994
ISBN: 0-940118-29-7
Excellent examples in the text and footnotes of the difficulties and variations in translation of the passages describing the building of Solomon's Temple. I have given special attention to the complex references to knots (eggs, animal heads), open flowers, chains and iron.

L'Italia in Africa
Tripolitania

Vol.I
Parte Prima
Istituto Poligrafico dello Stato P.V., Italy

1960

p. 29 "nodi di Salomone". **p. 38** "nodi di Salomone". **p. 40** "nodi di Salomone". **Tav. 7** Photo of mosaic floor at Sabratha with nodi di Salomone. **Tav. 35** Photo of mosaic floor at Sabratha with nodi di Salomone. **Tav. 42** Photo of mosaic floor at Sabratha with nodi di Salomone. **Tav. 47** Photo of mosaic floor at Tripoli with nodi di Salomone. **Tav. 55b** Photo of mosaic floor at Tripoli with nodi di Salomone. **Tav. 56** Photo of mosaic floor at Tripoli with nodi di Salomone. **Tav. 57** Illustration with nodi di Salomone. **Tav. 60** Photo of mosaic floor at Tripoli with nodi di Salomone. **Tav. 61** Photo of mosaic floor at Tripoli with nodi di Salomone.

Looking at European Ceramics
A Guide to Technical Terms

David Harris and Catherine Hess
The J. Paul Getty Museum
in association with British Museum Press
Malibu, California, London England
1993
ISBN: 0-89236-216-2

p. 26 Solomon's Knot on a tile decorated using the *Cuerda Seca* technique. **The authors comment that Cuerda Seca is a technique for decorating tile that was adopted by Spanish potters about 1500 from Near Eastern craftsmen. One more instance where the Knot design probably traveled in tandem with the technology.**

Magical Jewels of the Middle Ages
and the Renaissance, Particularly in England

Joan Evans, B. Litt.
Dover Publications, Inc.
New York
1976
ISBN: 0-0-486-23367-7

p. 22, etc. As a general reference for the enduring universal desire to endow objects, emblems and people with magical powers.

Medieval Panorama

Edited by Robert Bartlett
The J. Paul Getty Museum

Los Angeles
Thames & Hudson Ltd.
United Kingdom
2001
ISBN: 0-89236-643-5

pps. 238-239, plates 6, 7, 8 These pages feature comments on design, specifically interlaces, and cross cultural interaction. While the dating of interlaces offered may be valid as it relates to the three items shown, the notations fail to recognize basic history. Therefore the comments mislead as to the sequence of the cultures and the design influences they shared with one another.

While basic designs do have continuing cross cultural use, with Solomon's Knot being an early manifestation, the correct primary sequence of this first interlace is:

• INDIVIDUALS, PRE-FORMAL RELIGION

• VARIOUS EARLY BELIEF SYSTEMS

• JEWISH KING SOLOMON'S REIGN, CIRCA 900 B.C.E.

• CHRISTIANITY, FROM ABOUT 40 C.E.

• ISLAM, FOUNDED AFTER 648 C.E.

Metal Craftsmanship in Early Ireland
Dr. Michael Ryan
Town House and Country House, Dublin, Ireland
1993
ISBN: 0-946172-37-4

p. 27 An interlace used for the first time in Irish art in *The Book of Durran*, seventh century C.E.

Mexican Jewelry
Mary L. Davis and Greta Pack
University of Texas Press
Austin, Texas
1963
ISBN: 0-292-75073-0

pps. 183-189 Los Castillo. **plate 116** Solomon's Knot in married metals.

Mexican Silver
Penny Chittim Morrill and Carole A. Berk

Schiffer Publishing
Atglen, Pennsylvania
1994
ISBN: 0-88740-610-6
frontispiece *Platero, Codex Mendoza, Volume III*
p. 142 XII-3 The Knot on pins of silver, copper and enamel, by Antonio.

Moundbuilders
Ancient Peoples of Eastern North America
George R. Milner
Thames & Hudson
London
2004
ISBN: 0-500-28468-7
p. 137 figure 92 Artifact, hand with eye in palm. **p. 168 XIII** Hand of mica.

The Moundbuilders is a current, comprehensive and compassionate account of the Native Peoples of North America who lived in the woodlands and marshlands of what is now the Eastern United States. Building mounds of various shapes and sizes for burial and ceremony was practiced by these people for several thousand years. Exactly which people built mounds that circled or snaked over hundreds of acres has been a subject of debate since the mounds first attracted archaeological attention early in the nineteenth century C.E. Every sort of theory has been proposed, creating a circus of notions such as plays out around the giant Nazca ground images in Peru or the supposed UFO sightings in Roswell, New Mexico. Milner cuts through the hype, and presents the hard facts of their very hard life. He uses the discovery of hoards of artifacts of non-local materials to demonstrate the wide ranging systems of cooperation, competition and trade that persisted over the centuries.

The theory currently prevailing dismisses participation from Meso Americans in the Moundbuilders trade (even though there are artifacts that look very, very Mayan or Aztec), and I've become aware that suggesting European, Near, Middle or Far Eastern artistic influences is taken to be disparaging to the talents of any of the North American Native Peoples.

As an artist and artisan, with years of experience in my own and other design studios, I know that even good artists who create wonderful, original designs also pick up on design by others. So, it is probably more accurate to think that early North Americans were as alert and clever as today's artisans. Keeping this in mind while looking at a Moundbuilder's artifact, a hand with an eye in the palm, one can be permitted to notice that it looks an awful lot like the Hamsa, a Middle Eastern amulet for protection from the "Evil Eye". And one might dare to wonder if the *Solomon's Knot* motif that was stamped on Irene Site pottery for only about two hundred years might have filtered south from Viking contact, or come across the Bering Straits with the earliest Americans.

And even, (without jumping to conclusions, but letting one's mind run free,) just perhaps, the sacred symbols, hands, knots, stars, rosettes and fylfots, have made many journeys and return journeys to and from the Americas, carried by hand, brought ashore by ships or washed ashore from shipwrecks, on each occasion enriching the visual vocabulary of some artists, somewhere, artists who, in every case, somehow recognize them as spiritual metaphors.

Music for the Eyes
The Fine Art of African Musical Instruments
Los Angeles County Museum of Art, West and The Fowler Museum
Family Activity Guide
Bridget Cooks
Los Angeles
2000
Bronze bell worn by Yoruba chief to announce his approach. Nigeria, nineteenth century C.E. The bell is in the form of a head with a *Solomon's Knot* pendant around the neck. The text suggests that the pendant may represent the winding path that symbolizes life and death. The same bell is shown in a Fowler Museum catalog also noted in this bibliography with different text but a similar thought.

Music, Ritual, and Falasha History

Kay Kaufman Shelemay

Michigan State University Press

1989

ISBN: 0-87013-274-1

p. 17 *"...tracing their origin to Menelik, the fabled son of King Solomon and the Queen of Sheba.".* **p. 23** *"...Falashas, the fabled sons of King Solomon and the Queen of Sheba.".* **With extremely detailed first hand observations of Falasha practices, Shelemay attempts to document and interpret the true facts of their saga. While this very long history, hidden for millennia, is complicated and sometimes contradictory, the interaction between various faiths in Ethiopia is very clearly demonstrated. Symbols of several faiths or eras appearing on one amulet, such as crosses with Solomon's Knots is a perfect expression of that phenomenon.**

North American Indian Arts

Andrew Hunter Whiteford

Golden Press

New York

1970

Library of Congress Catalog Card Number 74-103423

p. 18 figure 1 Solomon's Knot stamped in clay. No reference is made to the North American, Native American Moundbuilders, but this piece seems to correlate with the known work of that culture.

oog ver kralen

Nelleke van der Zwan

Afrika Museum-Berg En Dal

1986

ISBN: 90-9400-209-4

p. 40, p. 13 English text translation. Yoruba twin figure wearing beaded jacket Solomon's Knot. The author puts forth a complex concept of the twin figure as a replacement for a real twin child who has died. The statue is cared for as a living child. Particularly relevant to this study is the statement that when the child has a jacket of beadwork such as the one pictured bearing a Solomon's Knot it is an indication that the child was royalty.

Oriental Rug Symbols

John Train
1998
ISBN: 0856674648
p.92   Two illustrations of the Knot, with the following explanations; The Knot is Destiny, also, in Islamic tradition knots may be tied to ward off evil, although a pilgrim entering Mecca must have no knots in his garments, and the Koran refers to sorcerers who tie magical knots and blow on them to cast spells.

Origins of the Bronze Age Oasis Civilization in Central Asia

Fredrik Talmage Hiebert
American School of Prehistoric Research
Bulletin 42
1994
Peabody Museum of Archaeology and Ethnology
Harvard University
Images 6, 7 Seals from the Margiana site in Central Asia.

Pictorial History of Philosophy

Dagbert A. Runes
Philosophical Library
New York
1959
p.103 Illustration of an astronomical apparatus of Hipparchus, its silhouette giving the appearance of a Solomon's Knot.

Primitive and Folk Jewelry

Edited by Martin Gerlach
Dover Publications, Inc.
New York
1971
ISBN: 0-486-22747-2
pps. 142-143 plate 34 Ornamental disc with Solomon's Knot, Middle Ages.

The Professor and the Madman

Simon Winchester
Harper Collins
New York
1998
ISBN: 0-06-017596-6

As a general reference, this book provides a vivid example of the human side of information gathering, documentation and interpretation.

Queen Elizabeth's Wardrobe Unlock'd

Janet Arnold
Folger Shakespeare Library, Washington DC
W. S. Maney& Son, Ltd.
Leeds, Great Britain
1988
ISBN: 0-901286-20-6
p. 3 figure 3 Detail of 'Lady Jane Grey' gown with *Solomon's Knot.* **p. 125 figure 191** Full portrait.

Sacred Realm

The Emergence of the Synagogue in the Ancient World
Edited by Steven Fine
Organized by the Yeshiva University Museum
Oxford University Press
New York, Oxford
1996
ISBN: 0-19-510225-8
p. 77 Aegina photo with *Solomon's Knot.* **p. 111** While many synagogue mosaic floors are featured, some of the photos or sketches selected for this book do not show the *Solomon's Knot* motif that appears in images of the same sites in other publications. I suggest that this once again shows that until the significance of this symbol is more generally recognized, editorial decisions may continue to inadvertently exclude this important source of information and interpretation.

The Standard Jewish Encyclopedia

Dr. Cecil Roth, Editor-in-Chief
Doubleday & Company, Inc.
Garden City, New York
1966
Library of Congress Catalog Number 62-15862
p. 168 Art, Jewish. **p. 716** Illustration of a mosaic floor in the nave of the synagogue at Gadera.

The Star of David: History of a Symbol

Excerpts from this book were given to me to read in 1985 by Rabbi Jacob Ott of Sephardic Temple Tifereth Israel, Los Angeles. I had consulted with him about my research on Jewish artisans, and my beginning quest for *Solomon's Knot*. The pages he sent to me were my first clue about how contested the names, shapes, and history of traditional Jewish symbols were among scholars. The Star of David seemed to be the focal point of the confusion, and while it is occasionally mentioned with a reference to *Solomon*, it seemed to me then as now, that more than enough attention was being paid to the Star, and that the *Knot* was the symbol that would be useful to explore. The reference book also contains some interesting information about the powers attributed to symbols. For example, the legend concerning *Solomon's* dominion over the spirits, including *Solomon's* signet ring inscribed with the unutterable name of G-d.

The Star of David Needlepoint Book

B. Borssuck
Arco Publishing, Inc.
New York
1979
ISBN: 0-668-04659-7
pps. 97-99
King Solomon's Knot diagrams for needlework.

Studies in the History and Archaeology of Jordan

Volume 3
Piccirillo
1989
p. 52, p. 168 figure 2.

Survey of Zairian Art

The Bronson Collection
Joseph Cornet
North Carolina Museum of Art, Raleigh, North Carolina
1978
ISBN: 0-88259-091-X
pps. 58, 61 figure 22, 224-225 figure 122 Kuba wood box with *Solomon's Knot,* labeled as an imbol knot interlace.

Tanach

The Stone Edition
The Torah/Prophets/Writings:
The Twenty Four Books of the Bible
Newly Translated and annotated
Edited by Rabbi Nosson Scherman
The Art Scroll Series
Mesorah Publications, Ltd.
1996, 1999
ISBN: 0-88906-272-5
Biblical Language scholar Jonathan Harris provided this information to me...
PEKAIM **when translated as flower or blossom, is actually using the image of an unopened flower, a bud or bulb. One Aramaic translation renders** *PEKAIM* **as egg. The translations are all related by shape, and the English translations evolve from Old English to modern usage, knop, knob, knot. French and Italian terminology reflects the English use of node or tree knot. But, whatever the variations in translations, the use of the word in Biblical Hebrew or Aramaic is consistent.**

Trades and Crafts in Medieval Manuscripts

Patricia Basing
The British Library
London
1990
ISBN: 0-7123-0187-9
pps. 49-52 plate iv Bankers. The pictured Solomon's Knots **completely covering a wall may be a reference to bankers with the symbol serving as $, or to dealers in precious metals, or to the religion of those dealers.**

Treasures of the Holy Land

Ancient Art from the Israel Museum of Art
The Metropolitan Museum of Art
New York
1986
ISBN: 0-87099-470-0
pps. 136-146 The Iron Age in King Solomon's time. **p. 214 figure 89** Drawing of main hall in first century C.E. mansion in the Jewish Quarter of Jerusalem, with ceiling border of Solomon's Knots.

Turn Up the Volume
A Celebration of African Music
Edited by Jacqueline Cogdell DjeDje
UCLA Fowler Museum of Cultural History
Los Angeles
1999
ISBN: 0-930741-76-5
p.273, catalog number 43 Bell. **p.336 catalog number 126** drum.

The Unending Mystery
A Journey through Labyrinths and Mazes
David Willis McCullough
Pantheon Books, a Division of Random House, Inc.
2004
ISBN: 0-375-42306-0
p.63 Speculation about King Solomon being the original source of the sacred geometry of labyrinths.

The Venetian Ghetto
Roberta Curiel, Bernard Dov Cooperman
Rizzoli
New York
1990
ISBN: 0-8478-1236-7
p.139 The Women's Gallery of the Levantine Synagogue, showing a stained glass window with Solomon's Knot.

Where Beads are Loved, Ghana, West Africa
Peter Francis, Jr.
Lapis Route Books
The Center for Bead Research
New York
1993
ISBN: 0-910995-15-X
Descriptions and photos relating to the manufacture and perception of Bodom Akoso beads appear throughout this twenty two page publication, and on the inside and outside back cover.

Yoruba Artist
Edited by Rowland Abiidun, Henry J. Drewal and John Pemberton III
Smithsonian Institution Press
Washington and London
1994
Ifa Trays from the Osogbo and the Ijebu Regions
Hans Witte
figures 4.13, 4.15, and 4.16 Depictions of carved wood divination trays and panels with many sacred symbols, including the Knot. In the treatise the Knot is referred to as *ibó*, and defined as the aspect of aristocracy.

Zaire 1938/39
Hans Himmelheber
Museum Reitberg
Zurich
1993
Image of scarification using Knot motif.

2,000 Designs, Forms and Ornaments
Compiled by Michael Estrin
Wm. Penn Publishing Corp.
New York
1947
pps. 25, 79-80, 123 Various Solomon's Knots.

periodicals and journals, listed by title

African Arts
UCLA
THE JAMES S. COLEMAN AFRICAN STUDIES CENTER
Volume xxxiv, Number 2, Summer 2001
More Than The Human Figure
The Marc and Denyse Ginzberg Collection of African Art
Article by Elizabet Cameron
photography by Lynton Gardner
p.54 plate EC Carved wood vase from the Kuba culture with Solomon's Knot motif. The attribution refers to the geometric design as *buina*.

Architectural Digest

Publisher, Knapp Communications Corporation

Los Angeles

January 1983

p.127 Photograph of a mosaic floor in Villa Kerylos, with large Solomon's Knot.

Beads, Journal of the Society of Bead Researchers

Karlis Karklins, SBR Editor

Ottawa, Ontario

Canada

2000-2001

Vols. 12-13

ISSN: 0843-5499

The Krobo and Bodom

Kirk Stanfield

p.72 Kirk Stanfield photo of a mold used by Krobo beadmakers to make the components used to decorate *akoso* beads, the beads with the Knot motif. The molds shown are more elongated Us or hairpin shapes, rather than J shapes, and the interlace sometimes appears on beads as an open ended figure. I wonder if the open and closed interlaces represent some artisans attempt at economy or efficiency, or if the two interlaces are actually understood by the Krobo beadmakers to have different meanings.

back cover, plates VIA and VIB Robert Liu photos include African and European made *akoso* beads.

Biblical Archaeology Review

July/August Volume 27 No.4

Yattir Mosaic

Hannan Eshel, Jodi Magness and Eli Shenhav

p.41 Diagram of the Yattir mosaic, with notes for each of the many symbols, except the two Knots. It is hard to understand why the Knot symbols seem to be invisible to archaeologists and anthropologists, but, as a student of beads I became familiar with this phenomenon of the *scientific blind spot*. For millennia beads have been made, worn, used, seen, depicted, but until the last part of the twentieth century they were almost never mentioned in print, similar in a way to the unnoted Knot.

Hebrew History Federation Ltd.

Samuel Kurinsky
New York
2001
Fact Paper 19-11 Jews in Africa
Part II Ancient Black African Relations

Sam Kurinsky had the right idea. To better understand symbols that appear on artifacts, it is important to understand the craftsmen who made them, and the traders who transported them. He devoted forty years to tracing evidence of Jewish artisans, and encouraging others to join in the research. This paper, with major input from George E. Lichtblau, a longtime Foreign Service officer for the U.S. Department of State in West Africa, documents in detail some of the Jewish influences to be found in various African cultures.

Hadassah Magazine

April 2002
New York
The Jewish Traveler: Gothenburg
Phyllis Ellen Funke

This article documents the Jewish presence in the port city of Gothenburg, Sweden. It includes a tantalizing description of the decorations in the old Great Synagogue, including side columns with braided and intertwined motifs that many claim resemble Viking or Celtic knots.

HaLAPID

The Journal of the Society for Crypto Judaic Studies
333 Washington Boulevard #336
Marina del Rey, CA 90292
Dedicated to filling in the facts of the Crypto Judaic experience in Spain, Portugal, and eventually all points. The publication is unique, meticulously researched and available to all scholars.

National Geographic Magazine

July 2001
Washington, DC
Keepers of the Faith, The Living Legacy of Aksum
By Candice S. Millard, Photographs by George Steinmetz
pps. 116-121

Native Peoples Magazine
September/October 2003
p.31 Drawing of a contemporary Native American necklace with six large *Solomon's Knots* surrounding a central stone inlay.

The New Yorker
Conde Nast Publications
New York
November 16, 1963
front cover
In a painting by Kovarsky of an Oriental rug gallery, a rug with Jewish symbols is shown, including *Solomon's Knots*.

Ornament Magazine
San Marcos, California
Winter 2001, Vol. 25 No. 2
Bodom and Related Beads
Robert K. Liu, Peter M. Ahn and Dudley Giberson
front cover and pps. 28-33.

Saudi Aramco World
Aramco Services Company
Houston, Texas
November/December 2001
Mosque Design in the United States
p.31 Window of mosque, Islamic Society of North America.
January/February 2005
p.31 Photo of mosque-madras complex of Sultan Hasan in Cairo, Egypt, with tiled *Knots*.

Southwestern Mission Research Center
Newsletter June 1996
A photo by Arnold Smith depicts two participants in a Pioneer Awards Ceremony, "Los Descendientes del Presidio", Fiesta de San Augustin, Arizona Historical Society, 1995. In the photo a young man, in what appears to be Spanish costume, carries a shield incised with a huge *Solomon's Knot*.

UCLA Alumni Magazine
Volume 15, No.3
UCLA Alumni Association
Los Angeles, California
February 2003
pps. 18-19
Building of Great Light
Reprinted from Westways Magazine September/October 2002
Building of Great Light
Powell Library is a 21st Century Alexandria
Robert Earle Howells text
Todd Masinter/Westways Magazine/Autoclub of Southern California

e-mail sources

k.williams@leonet.it
5/31/02
Verrocchio's Tombslab for Cosimo de Medici: Designing with a
Mathematical Vocabulary
Kim Williams writing on the Knot include *Il Nodo di Salomone*
Erba D'Arno, 60
Summer 1995
pps. 45-53
**In a response to my e-mail concerning the website, Kim
Williams commented that I was surely on the right track
with my investigation of** Solomon's Knot.

Libya
Libya and the Romans
Courtesy of Keith Daber
1987
Temporary file for *Libya*
A short, fact filled history of the country.

Republic of Ghana
http://www.ghana.com/republic/adinkra/symbols:html
Adinkra Symbols
5/27/02
p.1 Solomon's Knot is one of ten sacred symbols illustrated.
The translation of the meaning has to do with the intermingling
of the fake and the genuine.

symbols.com
3 pages
5/27/02
Notes regarding the hexagram, its historic uses and its various names, including several that refer to Solomon. While some of the notes might still be regarded as accurate, much of the dating is not informed. This is typical of most references now available, and is an example of why there is confusion regarding symbols, particularly Jewish symbols.

Thibauit.org/sca/scribe/classes/knotwork/
5/27/02
Diagrams for drawing Solomon's Knot.

miscellaneous sources

An interview with a Belgian mineralogist who lived in the former Belgian Congo.
This longtime resident of Africa recognized the Knot as a symbol that appeared on old coins in Katanga. He thought it might be the symbol for copper, or the equivalent of the $ sign. Many old Nigerian coins bear the Star of David. My interviewee drew the shape of the small coins he remembered and they had exactly the same shape as the large object that I had photographed at the Museum of the Congo in Brussels. It was covered with the Knot design. I show that photograph on the *Hunt for Big Names in Africa* page.

The Dohany Synagogue
Video produced by Tamas Barok & Doron Ritter
Hungary
contact +36-303435816
1998

Formatt No. 6623
Graphis Products Corporation
A sheet of rub-on symbols has the same square ended Knot that was found in a Latvian excavation, and a curved Knot such as the shape shown in my *Basic Shapes* page.

and finally...

C.G. Jung

The visionary psychoanalyst wrote that archetypes are perpetual vessels, continually filled and drained by the perceptions of each generation.

The C.G. Jung Institute of Los Angeles is near my home. I visited there as a result of inquiries from friends who were aware of Jung's interest in symbols. They had asked me if any reference to Solomon's Knot was present in his writings. I found no direct references, but I did find such spiritual warmth among the staff and attendees at the Institute's monthly programs that I returned several times. Jung's observation about archetypes seems to me to contain, for now and always, a truth for Solomon's Knot, as well as every other long lived symbol, drawn or dreamed.

Perpetual Vessels
Yoruba wedding baskets of glass beadwork and reeds,
each decoration a variation of Solomon's Knot.
Africa. Twentieth century C.E.

photography: Lois Rose Rose

Solomon's Knot has thousands of years of history, and this is the first study to begin to tell its magnificent, mysterious story. A listing of the relevant resources will always be a gathering in progress. After all the years of Knot appearances, the cue to document the titles on my bookshelf was startlingly clear...following six days of storms, my rain soaked ceiling fell to the floor and scattered plaster within one half inch of my computer, the Knot's computer. Within hours of that event my computer, my books, and my notes were moved and the work of securing the existing collection was begun.

Is to see
to be a seer?

If you know of,
do you know?

Will the seeker
be the finder?

Can the keeper
save and sow?

Solomon's
smiling!

OVER TIME, AS SOLOMON'S KNOT HAS BEEN ELABORATED UPON, THE WORDS TO DESCRIBE IT HAVE BECOME ALTERED, THE STORIES CONFUSED AND THIS SYMBOL OF FAITH ALMOST UNRECOGNIZED, UNTITLED, UNSEEN. THIS IS TRUE OF ITS DEPICTION AS WELL AS DESCRIPTION, AND SOMETIMES SEEING THE KNOT IS, IN THE SPIRIT OF SOLOMON, A RIDDLE...

THE RIDDLE MOSAIC
Two complete and five partial Solomon's Knots are in this antique Moroccan glass mosaic. With contrasting colored tiles at the intersections of the interlaces "Now you see 'em, now you don't."

photography: Lois Rose Rose

THANKS TO THOSE WHO HAVE RECOGNIZED THE KNOT, AND HAVE JOINED THE SEARCH FOR THAT WHICH IS EVERYWHERE...

FIRST, a wide ranging thanks to my flower filled city, Los Angeles, with its helpful librarians, gracious museum curators, stimulating and supportive arts organizations, ever interested collectors and inspiring clergy and educators.

NEXT, a loving thanks to my dear, dear friends and family who, be it a show or a birthday or a book, always offer hands-on help with enthusiasm and experienced good sense.

NOW...

Dr. Leslie P. Boston, editor par excellence, who asked the questions that made me see what I wanted to do.

Jim Robbins, sculptor of The Philosopher's Classic Form and Free Form. If Jim were a sandwich, he would be seasoned wit on wry.

Dr. James Lankton, who misses nothing, and shares it all.

Bessem Elias, artist and antiquarian, who provided me with books and introductions.

Jamey Allen, Beadman, who listened time and again.

Diana Friedberg, intrepid documentary film maker. We were perfect companions at the annual Tucson, Arizona Gem and Mineral shopping fantasy. There, Diana insisted that I could afford the Solomon's Knot royal beaded tunic, and that, in fact, I could not afford to pass it by. And she found the Celtic–Spanish porcelain with the Knot while she was filming in Galicia.

Samuel Kurinsky, my late, dear friend. Founder of the Hebrew History Federation, Sam provided me with facts, photos, and the very great benefit of his experience.

Robert Liu of Ornament Magazine. Robert has provided me and every other bead collector, researcher and artist with a cornucopia of information, inspiration, and encouragement.

Dr. Fred Krieger and Stella Krieger, who gave me The Mexican Silver book, its author, Penny Morrill, and even brought me a dashing Castillo.

Librarian Nora Matos, who remembered and researched the Merovingian Knot at Seviac.

Florine Sikking for all.

My Father, Robert Cole, who left to me an effective approach to any research; his favorite saying, "There are two reasons for everything, the good reason and the real reason."

Deborah Zinn, of BEADS-L and the Bead Data Base, who sent buttons.

Phyllis Gordon, non-stop traveler, who made her Uzbekistan purchased embroidered textile available to me.

Jonathan Harris, Jerusalem, for his bible translations, and his photos of Zippori's mosaics. Thanks also to his father, Michael Harris who shared the Zippori sighting and documentation.

The Bristols, and Bud's always ready camera as we traveled the Danube.

Karlis Karklins, Editor of the Journal of the Society of Bead Researchers. Karlis shared numerous sightings, his high standards and several "first, do no harm" readings of my work as it progressed.

Kaye D. Spilker of the Los Angeles County Museum of Art Textile and Costume Department, Curator of the lovely Erte/ Ballet Russes exhibition, who made inquiries for me about the exhibit's regal Knot decorated costume designed for the opera "Boris Godunov."

Molly Zachariash, Arts energizer, has often alerted me to the Knot in books, textiles, museum displays and art exhibits. And, it was Molly who found the Solomon's Knot mosaic kit in Tel Aviv.

Jeffrey M. Mitchem, President of the Society for Bead Researchers, who called my attention to sightings and to pitfalls.

Ellen Grim, for her Southwest sightings. Artist, collector and Teacher Supreme, she has shared her expertise with three generations in my family.

David H. Snow, Curator of Collections, Museum of New Mexico, Palace of the Governors, Santa Fe, New Mexico, for a candid interview and right-on referrals.

Arthur Benveniste, historian and Past President of the Society for Crypto Judaic Studies. As a result of his giving me a bit of time to speak at our San Antonio conference, an attendee sent an image of a Solomon's Knot covered tile wall in Lisbon, Portugal.

Eva S. Walsh, Florida, who designed and gifted me with a lovely glass seedbead Solomon's Knot.

Becca Licha, Santa Barbara, California, who made a Raku vase with an incised Solomon's Knot that demonstrates the elegant possibilities the Knot offers to modern artisans.

David Blume and Carolyn Hester for the comfort of David's expert reading, and the offering of a new melody for the ancient King.

Dirk Wales, who revisited the Powell Library at UCLA with me. And thanks to Dennis Bitterlich, a Powell Library archivist. He provided me with documentation about the Library, which was built in the 1920s and earthquake restored in the 1990s. True to "The Luck of the Knot" Dennis just happens to wear a wedding band circled by Solomon's Knots!

Rabbi Daniel Bouskila, of Sephardic Temple Tifereth Israel, Los Angeles, who inspires searching, researching and vision.

THE FRIENDSHIP TILES
Solomon's Knot glazed on antique Italian tiles.
A complex interlace, endlessly fascinating.

photography: Joel Lipton

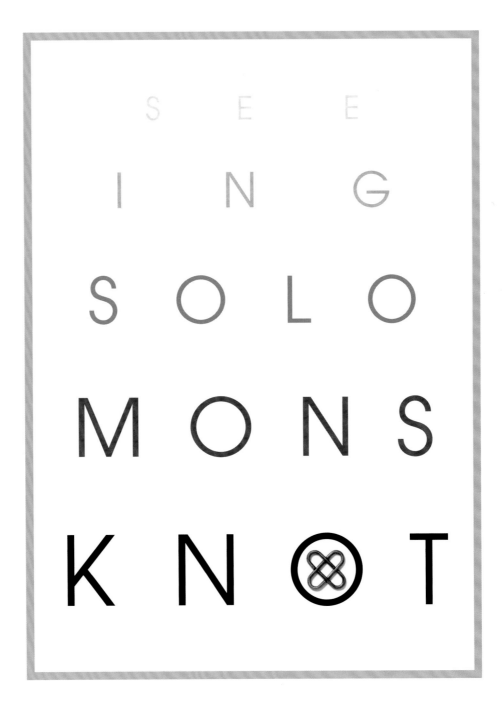

SEE
ING
SOLO
MONS
KNOT